the
COSMIC
TAROT

Jean Huets

the
COSMIC
TAROT

Illustrated by
Norbert Lösche

U.S. GAMES SYSTEMS, INC.
Publishers   **Stamford, CT 06902**

All illustrations, including cover, by Norbert Lösche
Cosmic Tarot deck © 1988 F.X. Schmid (Munich)
Vereinigte Münchener Spielkarten-Fabriken GmbH & Co. KG
Edited and designed by Jean Hoots
Library of Congress Catalog Card Number: 93-060978
ISBN 0-88079-699-5
10 9 8 7 6 5 4 3 2 1
Printed in the USA

U.S. GAMES SYSTEMS, INC.
179 Ludlow Street   Stamford, CT 06902 USA

CONTENTS

Contents

Contents

• Preface •

I WAS FIRST INTRODUCED TO THE TAROT in my student days. I can't remember how I heard of the cards, but I do remember that at the time, my friends and I were fascinated by the magic realm of archetypes, dreams, spells, symbols, psychism, numbers, the metaphysical plan of the universe. We went exploring—and we ended up in some very weird places: homemade maps of Dante's Inferno; kundalini color schemes applied to decor in order to effect mind alchemy; symbolic connections between nautilus shells, DNA, sound waves, and metaphysical trips (all considered spirals); rambling psychedelic poems; the Major Arcana assigned to the chapters of Thomas Mann's *The Magic Mountain;* amulets; voodoo paintings; Fellini and Cocteau films; spiritual fasts and vegetarianism coexisting with drinking parties and smoking; Cabalism coexisting with esoteric Roman Catholicism, Zen Buddhism, and Hinduism.

On graduating, our household moved to New York City. A job in occult publisher Samuel Weiser's bookstore (then on Broadway) was followed by a suffocating secretarial job at an academic publisher. A month's retreat in the Blue Ridge Mountains made me realize that I could not survive boring, respectable jobs. I was lucky on my return. Stuart R. Kaplan of U.S. Games Systems hired me as an editor—a job respectable but interesting.

I was in-house editor for about eight years, editing and researching books and booklets and corresponding with artists and authors. The biggest project was Volumes II and III of *The Encyclopedia of Tarot.* They were originally planned as one volume, but the mass of material demanded that we split the book.

After my husband and I moved to Virginia, I continued working free-lance as editor and book designer for U.S. Games

The Cosmic Tarot

Systems and others, as well as writing essays, fiction and drama, some of which has been published and produced under the same penname I have used for this book.

My tenure at U.S. Games Systems exposed me to a multitude of tarot decks and books, published and unpublished, from every corner of the world. I browsed through Stuart's fantastic library, volume by dusty volume, from Renaissance to contemporary, in order to form the bibliography for *The Encyclopedia of Tarot.* It was a slow process; many of the books hooked me in, and I confess that I spent time reading that I should have spent making entries in the bibliography. I corresponded with hundreds of artists, most of whose work can be seen in Volume III of *The Encyclopedia of Tarot.* Some artists produced deck after deck; one kind and inspired man, now deceased, visited our offices regularly, bringing new art every time. I also corresponded with the scholars of tarot, the men and women who are acknowledged in Volume II of the *Encyclopedia,* and had the great good fortune to meet many of them at a convention of the International Playing-Card Society. In researching the *Encyclopedia,* I grew absorbed in the people of the past who contributed to the tarot, from gamblers to occultists, from artists to aristocrats.

The human mind can take a million different journeys in a million different directions. The tarot, because of its adaptability, is a main road for many people. It is fascinating not only in itself, but also for its milieu, historically and currently.

Most impressive are the people who are deeply dedicated to tarot and to following their own light. A short, stout man came to our offices one day bearing a manuscript of 800-plus pages: a poetic tarot reflection on a vision that he had had of the Egyptian goddess Isis. We couldn't publish the work, but he wasn't surprised or dismayed—the epic was not yet complete, anyway. Having recently retired, he was taking a trailer trip up the East Coast with his wife, and decided to drop by our offices to share with someone what he'd produced. We enjoyed looking over the manuscript together. He was a most ordinary looking, extraordinary man. Whenever I'm depressed by television mass-mentality and conformity, I cheer myself up by remembering the people who pursue their own visions, no matter how far-fetched and impractical they may seem.

This book is dedicated
to all creative and inspired travelers,
past and present,
who have connected with the tarot.

• The Cosmic Tarot •

"So here we are, in the presence of the tarot, a book that is intentionally mute...." (Oswald Wirth, *Introduction to the Study of Tarot,* page 31)

THE TAROT IS A BOOK THAT SPEAKS THROUGH IMAGES; it speaks through our imaginations. It is rooted in silence: no one knows its origin.

Some claim the tarot is of Egyptian heritage; others trace it to India, the cradle of so much Western culture and wisdom now taken for granted. The images of traditional tarot decks are European and medieval. The Holy Roman Emperor and his consort appear.

Cards showing Pope and Popess led to the deck being censored or altered in Roman Catholic or, paradoxically, Protestant areas. (The Swiss replaced the offending cards with Jupiter and Junon.) The Wheel of Fortune was a well-known image during the Middle Ages, as was Death as a skeleton with a scythe.

The earliest extant tarot deck is from the Italian Renaissance; it was made around 1450 in Milan. The hand-painted, gold-leafed deck, with its charming, childlike figures, probably survives because of its artistic value. Any earlier decks were possibly discarded by people unaware of their value, burned if the local priest decided playing cards were "the devil's picture book," or destroyed in wars, especially during World War II, when aerial bombing leveled so much of the past.

Renaissance Italians and French enjoyed the game of tarot

The Cosmic Tarot

much as present-day folks enjoy bridge, except that the ladies shaved their foreheads and the gents wore stockings. Tarot, or tarock, is still a popular game in parts of Europe. Stuart R. Kaplan, a scholar and collector of tarot, and president of U.S. Games Systems, notes that while tarot decks were probably invented for a game, from very early on people were using the cards for telling fortunes and allegorical stories.

The first tarot decks may have been used for other purposes as well. The cards might have taught children principles of society and the cosmos. They were possibly esoteric codes of secret societies, alchemists, or witches. Gertrude Moakley claims they were pictures of Carnival parades, which descend from Roman triumphal parades (triumphs—trumps). Some say the images are based on the rites and deities of ancient goddess-centered religions. An interesting idea is that they illustrated the tales of the Round Table; the artist who made the earliest extant deck also made pen and ink drawings in a manuscript of Lancelot du Lac. They could also have been "fan magazines" of actors in pageants and plays. From the late Renaissance, decks printed by woodblocks were used for various games, mostly in France, Switzerland, and Italy.

The tarot eventually evolved into a form that is fairly consistent to this day. The traditional deck comprises seventy-eight cards. Twenty-two of the cards, numbered 0 through XXI, bear allegorical images and titles such as The Fool, The Empress, Justice, and The Star. These cards are called the Major Arcana, or the Trumps. The remaining fifty-six cards are called the Minor Arcana. They comprise four suits: swords, wands (staves or batons), cups, and pentacles (coins). Each suit has four court cards: king, queen, prince (traditionally, knight), and princess (traditionally, page); and numbered cards ace (one) through ten.

It was in the eighteenth century that the tarot evolved—for the first time, or once again—into an occult article. What follows is a brief chronology.

1781 A Frenchman, Court de Gebelin, stated that the tarot was Egyptian, the destroyed Library of Alexandria in code. He was a Mason, and something even more exotic—a powerful Protestant in France. Dozens of books have been based on his ideas, which in turn were based on "intuition," rather than on solid, scholarly research.

1783 The Book of Thoth tarot, the first "corrected" tarot, was created by Etteilla (Alliette, his surname, spelled backward). His deck was not traditional in that he altered the sequence of the Major Arcana.

1860s Eliphas Levi (real name, Alphonse Louis Constant) threw tarot into the magic cauldron of Cabalism, hermeticism, alchemy, and astrology.

1889 Papus (Dr. Gerard Encausse) published *Le Tarot des Bohemiens* (The tarot of the gypsies). The book included illustrations of the Major Arcana by Oswald Wirth, a disciple of the Marquis Stanislas de Guaita, one of the more formidable and sensational occultists of the nineteenth century.

1910 Pamela Colman Smith painted in watercolors the deck known as the Rider-Waite Tarot. The deck was named after Arthur Edward Waite, who guided the artist through the Major Arcana, and the first publisher of the deck, Rider of London. Like Etteilla, A. E. Waite claimed that his was a "rectified" tarot, that is, an occultly correct deck. It was based on the principles of the Hermetic Order of the Golden Dawn: a blend of Rosicrucianism, Cabalism, astrology, Masonic ritual, alchemy, and European mythology. Pamela Colman Smith was probably inspired by the designs of the late-fifteenth-century Italian Sola-Busca Tarot, copies of which are housed in the British Museum. The Sola-Busca Tarot is the only known early tarot deck whose Minor Arcana show scenes instead of symmetrical arrangements of suit symbols. The original artwork of the Rider-Waite Tarot disappeared after World War II, as did the original Sola-Busca Tarot, which was in Milan. By coincidence, they may have shared the fate of so much other art: casualties of war.

1927 Oswald Wirth published *Le Tarot: Images du Moyen Age* (The Tarot: Image-creators of the Middle Ages). The book included a portfolio of lovely, gold-illumined prints of the Major Arcana. These were modified from his illustrations for Papus's book. (The Oswald Wirth Tarot deck that is currently in print was made from copies of Wirth's designs.)

1940 Aleister Crowley, after breaking away from the Hermetic Order of the Golden Dawn, worked with painter Lady Frieda Harris to create the Book of Thoth Tarot. The deck was not published until 1969.

Hundreds, possibly thousands of different tarot decks are now in print around the world. The vast range of tarot decks points to the fact that tarot aficionados also vary: from collectors and artists to mystics and magicians, to psychics and psychother-apists, to herbalists . . . and on and on. Occultists use the tarot for predictions, in ritual, and as "flash cards" for whatever sys-tem—cabalistic, alchemical, quasi-Christian—they might wish to study. Mystics use the tarot for meditation and, overlapping the occultists, for advancement in other-worldly realms. Students of psychology can see in the figures of the tarot human types, ele-ments of the psyche, and archetypes.

Predicting is the most ridiculed aspect of the tarot. Many people who collect and study the tarot refuse to use it for telling the future. However, even the most hardened cynic will sit for a free reading or will even pay for "spiritual advice." They may slouch back with arms crossed on their chests and a meant-to-be cynical smile on their lips—but they want to know.

The tarot can put in images a life situation, in the same way that journal-writing can bring pattern and order to strong feelings and life's experiences. The randomness of a tarot reading forces the imagination to look at alternatives, to see things from a different perspective.

How are the cards interpreted? Everyone relies on books and booklets at first, and tradition plays a legitimate role in reading the tarot. But there comes a time when you must put the books aside, along with preconceptions and worries about whether or not you are psychic. Having absorbed the traditions, you personalize them by understanding the cards through context, considering the question asked or the situation.

The cards have different meanings for different people, in different situations. In a "psychological" reading, for example, the Emperor could be a helpful, older man, or he could be an aggravating employer/husband/father/friend. If you're a mature man, he might be you. Then again, if you're a mature, powerful, "masculine" woman, he might be you. If you work in a government building, the Emperor could symbolize your job or place of employment. What fits with the other cards? With your question? With the story?

A tarot reading brings together the eccentric theories as well as the scholarly research on the origin of the tarot, and the meanings that contradict, and the tremendous attraction of the tarot.

The tarot accommodates all readers; it can absorb any system. That is why many say the Egyptians invented tarot—after all, Thoth was a Magician, and Isis was a Popess, a High Priestess. Renaissance Italians could have invented the tarot, including in its ranks the Pope and the Holy Roman Emperor, and figures of the court. The tarot really seems to be an alchemical work—Temperance depicts an angel mixing fluids. Astrologers love the tarot: Libra is Justice, and there is Aquarius on The Star. Published and unpublished feminist decks abound: Strength is a woman, the Popess is the Goddess, and the Empress is the Matriarch. Jungians. . . . It goes without saying.

In the end, it is beside the point, except for historical purposes, to shoot down the occult myth that has grown up around the tarot. Obviously, ancient Egyptians had nothing to do with creating the tarot. Yet the tarot has been used successfully to illustrate the figures of ancient Egyptian religion. And whether the original author of the tarot was Thoth or Hermes, or a minor artist of the Renaissance making a deck for the weekend card game at the palàzzo, the tarot is, indeed, a magical book. Magical in that it can change into all different forms. A book in that each image tells its story. A magical book: it is written even as you read it.

The Cosmic Tarot, with its fascinating, intricate images, reflects all that the tarot has been, and all that it can be. Its symbolism ranges freely through time, from ancient Egypt to present-day Europe. We can identify with the human figures, whether they are in the costume of the pharaohs or in modern business suits. Noble or abject, wise or enchained in folly, free-spirited or snared in materialism and decadence, the people on the deck show us ourselves in the midst of life. Both the familiarity and the mystery of the figures draw us in, into ourselves, into pondering the questions that recur over and over in our lives.

The artist of the Cosmic Tarot, Norbert Lösche, deliberately chose recognizable images. Says Lösche, "In creating this tarot, my intention is to make the old knowledge accessible and understandable to everyone by using as few secret symbols as possible…. In our times, the search for transcendent meaning and self-redemption has replaced the old mystical religions of a distant god. The tarot's age-old knowledge is always quiet and reserved, yet it welcomes the seeker like an old friend. The tarot, with its dynamic concept of constant change, offers a doctrine for the New Age and thus becomes a reliable guide in this chaotic world of shifting social values."

Imagination

"Methodical observations, experiment, and calculation
have led us to such results that we silence our imaginations when they try to suggest anything to us. This is
being far too careful because intuition has such an important part to play in life that it is absurd to try and turn it
into an abstraction. Rather than suppressing them
fearfully, it would surely make more sense to develop our
imaginative faculties under the control of reason."
(Oswald Wirth, *Introduction to the Study of Tarot*, page 49)

Sit in a comfortable, quiet place. Pick up the Cosmic Tarot deck
and scan the images one by one. Look at each card for a few
seconds; resist pausing over any one in particular. As you glance
at the cards, try to be aware of your emotional reactions, of your
flying thoughts, of associations. Perhaps a face recalls someone
you know—a friend or an enemy. Perhaps one card is sinister,
another sunny and pleasant.

This exercise in image-ination can be almost psychedelic, as
the rapid succession of images gives rise to a dazzling variety of
thoughts and emotions.

Now put the deck down and examine your mind. Don't measure or judge your impressions in terms of good or bad, psychic
or mundane. Merely try to recall the general flow of your
thoughts and feelings as you scanned the deck.

You probably found that you couldn't help but stop on certain
cards. Perhaps an image was beautiful; perhaps an image was
revolting or frightening; perhaps an image puzzled or intrigued
you. The attractive cards as well as the repulsive cards can reveal
aspects of your psyche. Over time, your feelings toward certain
cards will go through surprising changes.

Each tarot card, Major or Minor Arcana, represents a facet of
life. We may identify with certain cards—for example,
young-at-heart people or people just meeting the tarot tend to

The Cosmic Tarot

identify with 0 The Fool. We may match people we know with certain cards. Remember, however, that each card is only a piece of the picture, part of the story.

As you look through the Cosmic Tarot deck again and again, contemplating one card at length, passing over those that are unpleasant or of little interest, try always to be aware of your "flying thoughts." These are the inspirations that will, as you study the tarot, be captured and given form by reason. This created/creative form is the treasure that the tarot has to offer.

• The Major Arcana •

THE MAJOR ARCANA OF THE TAROT SYMBOLIZE, as the name implies, the "big picture." They can be seen in numerical order as a journey through life: from 0 The Fool, the blissfully ignorant embryonic child, to XXI The World, the liberated and liberating integrated person, portrayed as a mature woman joyous in the midst of life. They can be read as a picture book of metaphysics: from 0 The Fool, uncreated potential, to XXI The World, full manifestation.

The Cosmic Tarot book interprets each Major Arcana card first with a description of the image on the card. The description is brief. Visual study of the card will yield the discovery of details that contribute to one's own relationship with it. Following the description is a section called "The Cosmos," a macrocosmic outlook on the card. Next, "The Human Community" views the card as a facet of human society and civilization. "The Individual" brings the card down to personal terms, showing life situations and types of people. Finally, simple meanings are given for each card. The meanings are often contradictory; what works well in one situation, for one person, can work badly in another situation, for another person.

Reversed meanings (for when the cards fall upside down in a spread) are not given. Each card is interpreted according to its image and context. If one feels that the positive (or negative) value of the card is stymied, compromised, or blocked by surrounding cards or by the subject of the reading, an unfavorable (or favorable) interpretation might be indicated.

The sections are not meant to imply that metaphysics, society, and personal life are divided and shut-off from each other. The aspects of life blend with and influence each other. The delineations of "The Cosmos," "The Human Community," and "The Individual" can help us to see the wondrously various ways in which the energy denoted by each card touches our lives. What connects with our spirits can benefit our bodies, our spiritual well-being is woven into our society, and so on.

Finally, in reading the interpretations and descriptions of the cards, it is essential to understand that the pronouns "he" and "she" are used in reference to the gender of the figure on the card. The actual qualities of the cards are not gender-bound, except for a few cases noted in the text. For example, though the Magician is called "he," the type described can be a man or a woman; however, the Magician refers sometimes specifically to a brother, a male friend, or an ordained man.

THE FOOL

0 The Fool

A jester in motley dances at the edge of a cliff. A dog, symbol of fidelity, leaps beside him, perhaps warning him of the dangers of the deep. The sun inspires the Fool with spheres of light. Crystals grow from the ground.

The Cosmos The number 0 is the mathematical point of neutrality between positive numbers and negative numbers. In metaphorical terms, the Fool is the point of balance between destruction and creation. S/He signifies the held breath of the cosmic force: the exhalation is creation; the inhalation is annihilation. The Fool is spirit on the edge of manifestation; the formless who precedes or succeeds the dualism of heaven and earth; "ground zero," the bomber term for the center of destruction. An absolute neuter, neither male nor female, neither active nor passive, the Fool embodies in its circular digit all possibilities.

The Human Community The Fool, or court jester, is wise in folly, witty in madness. Alone in the court, he candidly exposes the king's foolishness, with the king's consent and even with his encouragement.

We have in ourselves the capacity to satirize our own foolishness, to laugh at ourselves and to laugh at the folly of our leaders—even as they, like the Fool, bring us dancing to the edge of a precipice. A humorless life would be unbearable, and our professional jesters—cartoonists, comedians, clowns, and essayists—keep our leaders from taking themselves too seriously, and keep us from taking our leaders too seriously.

However, pretending that life is nothing but a joke, refusing to confront responsibility for ourselves and our actions, eventually leads to destruction and chaos. Complacent cynicism makes fools of us. Closed eyes bring us over the precipice, led by the fantasies of those who would dominate us.

The Fool is the short-term solution, the easy way out: public vaccinations and education on disease control vetoed; shoddy safety standards to favor low production costs; exploitative labor practices to compete with other economies; using human rights as a public relations facade in swapping political favors. Sooner or later, the precipice—pollution, epidemics, revolution, civil suits by injured workers or consumers—will gape open.

Conversely, the Fool is the activist, the dissenter, the one who forces us to face social problems even if solving them seems impractical politically and economically. He may be a "Chicken Little," or he may be a prophet.

The Individual Imagination is a sister of ecstasy, and ecstasy is a razor's edge between sanity and insanity. The most heartbreaking delusions and the most exquisite beauty spring from imagination.

The Fool embodies the imagination, with all its glamour and all its danger. His head reaches toward the sun and the stars; his feet caper on the very lip of a crystal-studded alpine cliff. He is the romantic artist who creates universally loved masterpieces; he is the madman who makes no sense to anyone but himself.

It is appropriate that the Fool is the 0, the naught, for the imagination by itself signifies nothing. Only when given form does the imagination make an impact. However unstable an "artistic type" may be, creation will always include a fair measure of solid, calculating reason. The faithful dog dances along, but keeps the Fool from losing awareness of the surroundings.

The imaginary excursions that lead to creation can be spontaneous, even "foolish." The nineteenth-century chemist Friedrich August Kekulé von Stradonitz was dozing on an omnibus one day when he "saw" atoms twirling about in a dance. The end of a chain of atoms joined itself to the head of the chain and made a whirling ring. The playful vision immortalized Kekulé von Stradonitz, as it was a breakthrough realization in modeling the structure of benzene and led to models of other cyclic chemicals.

A person who is too much in love with reason and purposefulness, one who is incapable of wasting time, will never know the joy of creation. Fascist or totalitarian societies require that artists fill the "needs of the people," which usually means finding the lowest common emotional and political denominator—nothing risky, nothing experimental or offensive. These societies label as "decadent" the artist who creates for the joy of it, for "art's sake." The wish to conform to what society dictates as sensible and productive (and lucrative) is a more effective censor than any government bureau.

The Fool is a youth, male or female, or a youthful spirit. He or she may be thoughtless, even callous, but always brings that welcome breath of fresh air. All creative endeavors, especially those that make us laugh, are in the domain of the Fool, as are mimes and clowns of all kinds, from class clowns to professional buffoons to the benevolent Shriners. The Fool is possibly a bumbler, the person who always commits the faux pas, the one who "spills the beans."

Meanings: Wisdom of innocence. Originality. Annulment of reason. Frivolity. Lack of discipline. Ecstasy. Delirium. Satire. Cartoons. Clowns. Mime. Madness. Imagination. Youthfulness. Comedy. Fun. Lack of social grace. Thoughtlessness. Folly. Extravagance. Immaturity. Irrationality. Frenzy. Enthusiasm. Naiveté.

THE MAGICIAN

I The Magician

The Magician's face has both masculine and feminine features: moustache and goatee, delicate eyebrows and mouth. S/He wears a fillet decorated with the lemniscate, used in mathematics to signify infinity. Through mental powers, s/he rules the four elements—the four suit signs of the tarot. The roses of passion and the lilies of purity are near the table.

The Cosmos The Roman numeral I is identical to the Roman letter I, which signifies the self-aware ego in English. "I" is oneness, and also "only-ness." The lonely One craves a reflection, which will be identical and yet opposite; the potential of 0 The Fool coalesces into a creative force: God/Goddess, Life, Breath, Love, Inspiration, Mind, the Great One. The presence of the four suit signs indicates that from formlessness have come the elements of form. The Magician is Form, then, and his sister the High Priestess is Time.

The sword, wand, cup, and pentacle symbolize the four elements of life as understood by the human mind: respectively, air/mental, fire/spiritual, water/emotional, and earth/physical.

The Human Community The Magician manipulates the elements to invent, to create, to cast a spell, and so he rules innovation and pioneering work: research and development, experimental or avant garde art, and radical sociology. His work has the potential to fulfill the needs of humans, though he is neutral as to the moral implications of its uses. Thus, dynamite can be used to excavate building sites or it can be used in bombs. The roses denote passionate dedication; the lilies represent pure, single-minded devotion.

The Magician manipulates people as well as the elements. Charismatic, attractive, and persuasive, he knows how to play all the chords, charming us mentally, spiritually, emotionally, and physically. The Magician is the priest and the leader—and the charlatan, the pretender. The audience that forgets the illusory quality of the show is duped. The priest or preacher who claims for himself the qualities of the spirit he worships is a charlatan. The vote-buying promises of politicians are the magic tricks that veil the real difficulties involved in governing.

The Magician can reflect the tendency of groups to get caught up in the power, charisma, or promises of an individual. Such situations have led to the founding of great religions such as Islam, Buddhism, and Christianity, and have also led to brain-washing cults and the most savage tyrannies, such as those under Adolph Hitler and Idi Amin.

The Individual The Magician is the ideal person to raise funds for a cause, to convert or persuade a difficult audience, to solve a complex problem through sheer ingenuity. Once the trick is done, however, his interest wanes. Someone else will have to follow through. He is interested in seeing how his work is applied, but most likely needs a business partner, unless he himself has the means of production. Potential investors may be alienated by the fact that he doesn't always play by the rules.

Though not necessarily immoral, the Magician is not scrupulous. He will not agonize over the consequences his work may have. His means support the end; the process, not the goal, is all. One result of his detachment is the ability to dedicate himself to a task that may have no material reward or status. The other side of scholarly detachment is science gone amok: cruelty to

animals, the invention of devastating weapons. The Magician can
be a heartless playboy or playgirl, making a science of seduction
and abandoning his or her subject when the experiment has
yielded results; or the Magician's objectivity can allow him to love
unpossessively a free-spirited person.

The Magician can be a brother, a friend of long-standing, or
an ordained man. He can be tremendously supportive or mad-
deningly competitive. If the Magician is in the form of a woman,
she will gravitate to traditionally male jobs and roles.
The Magician rules crackpots whose great ideas never make it
off the drawing board, inventors, con artists, sleight-of-hand
artists, "Mr. or Ms. Fix-its," master artisans, and artists who con-
centrate more on style and form than on content and meaning.

Meanings: Brother or friend. Elementary knowledge. A free
spirit. Determination. Skill. Juggling. Initiative. Agitation. Disgrace.
Self-reliance. Intelligence. Inventiveness. Self-confidence.
Resourcefulness. Deception. Sleight of hand. Clumsiness. Egoism.

THE HIGH PRIESTESS

II The High Priestess

The High Priestess is marked with oceanic tides; the starry cosmos mingles with her hair. The blue tint of her hair and skin denotes restfulness and depth. On her forehead is a yin-yang symbol: union and dualism. A book imprinted with the first and last letters of the Greek alphabet is before her. The crescent moon, which governs the tides, shows the High Priestess to be in harmony with the ebb and flow of life and death.

The Cosmos The High Priestess, in anticipation of the matronly Empress, is often called virginal. Her womb has the potential to nourish a living being, but if conception is denied, menstruation brings the demise of the unfertilized ovum. The life force comes in its time to each being and withdraws in its time, just as ocean tides come and go, just as the moon waxes and wanes.

The yin-yang denotes the fundamental truth of nature as perceived by humans: that all energy is generated by the interplay of opposites, the alternation of negative and positive, light and dark, dry and wet, hot and cold, day and night.

The letters alpha and omega, inscribed in the book, are the first and last letters of the Greek alphabet. As her brother the Magician coagulates the elements to make creation possible, the Priestess takes from eternity time: beginning and end.

The Human Community The Magician represents the application of knowledge; the High Priestess represents

17

knowledge itself. She is the ivory tower. Theories on the origin of the cosmos, the most hair-splitting semantic argument, Mandelbrot sets, are all of interest to the High Priestess. Some of the data she turns up will eventually be used by the Magician; for example, the Mandelbrot sets can help pinpoint chaotic elements in models of shoreline erosion. Meanwhile, the Priestess will always have a fascinated, if elite, audience.

The High Priestess also represents the unofficial side of world religions (compare with V The Hierophant). Established churches have always been uneasy with their saints, visionaries, and reformers, but the community of any religion becomes a mere reflection of the worldly status quo without creative, and some-times obsessed, individuals. Saint Francis of Assisi, Thomas à Kempis, and Tibet's Milarepa, and especially women such as the bodhisattva Tara, Joan of Arc, and Hildegard of Bingen reflect the kind of energy symbolized by the High Priestess. They did not start religions. They used existing institutions to realize unique visions. The High Priestess is the abbess or leader of obscure religious communes or orders that have only tenuous connec-tions with established churches.

The Individual The High Priestess attracts men and women, though she tends to be reserved and unassuming, even cold. She may be a "bookworm." One could say of her, "still waters run deep." The High Priestess can indicate a feeling of certainty, even if various aspects of a situation are yet hidden.

The High Priestess is the older or younger sister: an intimate relationship bound by taboos. She may be a beloved female friend or an ordained woman. If the High Priestess takes the guise of a man, he will be somewhat effeminate and very under-standing of women.

The High Priestess can represent a young, virginal woman, or a woman who has control of her sexuality in terms of activity and fertility. In this respect, she can denote successful birth control.

Meanings: Mystery. Hidden knowledge. Wisdom. Sound judgment. Common sense. Serenity. Penetration. Foresight. Intuition. Initiation. Mental power. Silence. Perception. Self-reliance. Sister. Impassiveness. Quiet assertiveness. Platonic relationships. Love of books. Shallowness. Obsessiveness. Passive–aggressive type.

THE EMPRESS

III The Empress

A mature woman crowned with stars, rich with jewels, rules a fertile land. Around her neck is a pendant on which is a five-pointed star. The pentagram is a symbol of the five senses as well as of wealth and the earth; it appears in the suit of pentacles of the Minor Arcana.

The Cosmos The Empress is the Great Mother, the physical form of creation, what we perceive with our senses as the cosmos. She gives from her own body as a mother gives milk to her infant. We dwell on her body; we draw our food from her body. We admire her beauty when we look up at a starry sky. Wind, clouds, rain, sunshine are from her. We dance and love on her body—we also defile her body.

While the Mother seems endlessly nurturing, endlessly forgiving, there is a point at which her resources give out: for examples, the Dust Bowl of the United States, a semi-arid region formed in the 1930s by over-cultivation of the land; the extinction or endangerment of countless species of plants and animals; the decimation of rain forests. From time to time, too, she devours her own: volcanoes, earthquakes, the devastating 1986 natural eruption of lethal vapor from Cameroon's Lake Nyos, cancer from too much exposure to sunlight.

The Empress card emphasizes the gift of life. A bird in the foreground clasps a berry in its beak; the earth feeds her children, winged, finned, and legged. The fertility of the earth is illustrated by the globe that floats amidst ripe stalks of grain and wild flowers. The mountains in the background recall the favored meditation grounds of sages. Mountains are the earth laid bare.

The Human Community The Empress is the ecosystem of civilization: farmlands, fishing and hunting grounds, mines, timberland, parks, and gardens—all natural resources used by humans. Both the beauty and the perils of cultivation and husbandry are implicit in the Empress. She is exquisite gardens and beloved animal companions, as well as strip-mined mountainsides and smoggy skies.

Historically, all over the world, nature has been seen as a force to be subjugated, dominated, exploited. (The parallel with the roles of men and women is obvious.) For example, the creator in the Hebrew book of Genesis commanded man to subdue the earth and dominate its life.

The ecology movement offers a different point of view. A stewardship role obliges humankind to protect earth's resources and to use them only if they are able to be preserved and/or regenerated. The concept is workable, and probably most realistic at this point in time. Stewardship does not relinquish the paternalistic idea of human rulership over nature, but at least the power exerted is meant to be benevolent, rather than greedy, destructive, or negligent.

Humankind must arrive at an agreement with nature. She is not "other," outside of ourselves. Nature is humanity, and conflict with her is suicide. The Empress personifies the vital interdependence of humankind and nature.

The Individual The Empress is our mother—real or ide-
alized. She may be literally a mother, or she may be a motherly
person, male or female. She believes in her progeny, no matter if
the whole world is opposed, and she will always be supportive
and encouraging, ready to lend a hand. With loyalty that borders
on ferocity, she guards her own. The Empress can help us grow,
or she can stunt us with overprotectiveness: smothering rather
than mothering.

A tendency to be materialistic can make the Empress
exploitative. She indicates wealth, especially wealth gained
directly from natural resources.

The Empress loves nature, generally not in rugged majesty
but as made comfortable for human activities: gardening, easy
hiking trails, parks, horse riding, zoos, fishing, bird watching,
crafts using natural objects, camping in spring and fall, recreational
beaches, and so on. She is fond of food and loves to cook for
others. Her home is the gathering place for family, whose members may be her friends as well as her children and relatives. The
Empress can indicate an unexpected pregnancy or, conversely, a
planned pregnancy.

Meanings: Feminine wisdom. Feminine power. Fruitfulness.
Sensuality. Beauty. Culture. Abundance. Accomplishment.
Mother. Wife. Fertility. Feminine influence. Ability to motivate
others. Practicality. Boredom. Lethargy. Temptation through
earthly things. Gluttony.

IV The Emperor

The Emperor is enthroned, the symbols of his power before him. The scepter is the rod of chastisement whereby rebellion is quelled; the orb signifies the universal extent of the Emperor's dominion. In the background is a lush, walled garden. The Emperor's love and care flowers the earth. Just beyond the wall are the sands of the desert. The displeasure of the ruler is the waste of war and neglect. Pyramids, the giant tombs of the pharaohs, rise from the desert.

The throne of the Emperor is the seat of power. Two rams' heads surmount it, symbolizing the astrological sign of Aries, head of the zodiac. The starry night sky edges the chair.

The Cosmos Whereas the Magician is the creative Mind, the Emperor is the sustaining Mind. Husband to Nature the Empress, he and she are interdependent, unable to exist without each other. The Empress is the wind and the phenomena, such as hot and cold, moisture and dryness, that make the wind blow. The Emperor is neither cause nor result: he is what unites the result and its causal phenomena. The Emperor is natural law.

The Human Community The Empress is the natural infrastructure of society; the Emperor is the rules by which resources are used and distributed: the power structure and the status quo. He may symbolize a ruler elected or self-appointed, a government, or the collective will of a people, especially in nationalistic terms.

The Emperor's raised eyes indicate ambition: to improve the condition of his subjects, to create a more equitable system of government, or to extort more wealth from his subjects and to force his rule on peoples and lands beyond his proper realm. In essence, the Emperor is authority and the determination to mould the world in accordance to the will.

The Emperor signifies government buildings, such as the United States Capitol and the English Houses of Parliament, and national monuments and memorials. The urge to build, to govern, to colonize, to incorporate, to act out philosophies of government are in Emperor's realm. Danger may come in crossing his dynamic, imperialistic ambition.

The Individual   The parent, the dictator, the schoolteacher, the elected official are the Emperor. Self-discipline and self-imposed rules are also the Emperor.

Whether the Emperor is an internal or external figure, he can be a source of great strength and resourcefulness. He is the means to carry out ideas and plans. He can be a ruthless master, though, the tyrannical parent who verbally or physically beats the self-esteem out of his children, or he can be the parent within, the overweening superego that represses trust, spontaneity, sensuality, and creativity.

The Emperor may indicate a dynamic, take-charge person, one who can galvanize an apathetic group into becoming an active force. His strength of character can lead to a rather harsh or cynical attitude toward those who do not live up to his high principles.

Meanings: Shaping the material world. Rulership. Will. Severity. Stability. Governmental structure. Worldly power and its danger. Force. Confidence. Discipline. Strength of character. Wealth. Authority. War-making tendencies. Father. Husband. Patriarchal figure. Weakness of character. Pettiness. Abuse of power. Corruption. Imperialism.

V The Hierophant

A religious leader stands in a temple, his followers at his side. His crown is faced with the sun; one horn of the crescent moon is visible. In his right hand he holds a card that is pierced by the light ray of his vision. In his left hand is another card; it is from the Cosmic Tarot deck, but only the back can be seen. A dove flying among the pillars of the church is symbolic of the spirit. The light that bends around the Hierophant is generated by an ankh, Egyptian symbol of life. Two green banners that edge the image symbolize the presence of nature, even in the most refined temples. The cosmos is visible through the openings of the stone.

The Cosmos Some people see in the starry night constellations; some see a chaos of lights. A scientist takes fossils as proof of evolution on earth; a fundamentalist Christian may consider those same fossils to be snares put down by the devil in order to delude humankind into discounting the Genesis account of creation. Each believer considers his or her own belief system to be the absolute truth.

The Hierophant is a paradox of differing points of views: pattern or chaos; divine law or random circumstances; evolution or creation. He does not cause anything to happen; he is not creative. One could say he is a figment of the mind: the cosmos as we see it. As ordinary mortals, we are too conditioned to understand the true nature of things, and we cannot create anything

new. We can only speculate, and re-form the materials we have
in our realm.

The Human Community   The male followers of the
Hierophant are dressed in "church clothes," one in an outfit that
resembles a cardinal's gown and cap, except that it is blue, and
the other in black gown and white collar. They represent the
conventional side of religion: dogma, ethics, hierarchy, scripture,
as well as the speculations of theology and cosmology.

The women are more unorthodox. Their gold hoop earrings
give them a gypsy flavor. The white headcovering worn by the
foremost woman recalls the veils worn in church by Roman
Catholic women up into the sixties, but now abandoned by most
Western women. The starry headdress decorated with a feather,
worn by the other woman, hints at the imagination's flight in the
cosmos. The women are the unconventional side of religion:
visions, practices abandoned or banned by religious authorities,
creation of personal rituals, intense and single-minded devotion,
the blending of indigenous and colonial religions.

Established religion has its place. Not everyone can be a mystic, a hermit, or a leader. Some degree of stability is beneficial for
most people, and many appreciate the guidance of tradition and
dogma. Religions such as Roman Catholicism and Tibetan
Buddhism value lineages of sages (such as the pope and the Dalai
Lama), who confer on their followers knowledge and sacramen-
tal practices.

The Hierophant as church ideally protects solitary travelers as
well as guiding those who wish to follow a more populated road. He
can provide the ground for spiritual practice, as well as a guide to
ethical behavior. In that respect, the Hierophant symbolizes the
prevalent morality of a social group. He can also drop the seeds
for neurotic guilt, intolerance, and an unhealthy suppression of
natural appetites and instincts. Faith can be mindless conformity,
or it can be an experience that bypasses intellectualization and

The Cosmic Tarot

selfish calculation to come truly from the heart. Church buildings, meditation centers, mosques, temples—the physical structures of religions—are indicated by the Hierophant.

The Individual The Hierophant is a priest, preacher, teacher, friend, or group of kindred spirits who connects with us in prayer and meditation, or in philosophical or ethical quests. He is likely to be a member of a conventional religion or faculty at an academic institution. His use of ritual is always elegant and effective, even if the ritual consists only in taking a certain posture to pray, such as kneeling or sitting cross-legged. One of the Hierophant's more extraordinary qualities is the ability to communicate directly with individuals, even while teaching a large group.

Possibly the Hierophant is an opportunist who uses his status to draw material and sexual favors from his students. He may relish the power to save or damn those who fall under his spell or the spell of the doctrine he preaches.

A true spiritual teacher, male or female, is a friend. As a friend, he accepts us as we are, not as robotlike, brainwashed cultists. An authentic teacher discourages blind faith and dumb compliance. Trust is not a demand, but rather a natural, growing part of the relationship. Once a metaphysical bond is established between teacher and student, it is never broken. The teacher will never give up on the student; the student will never lose the teacher, even in death.

We can see the Hierophant as one who leads us on the path to spiritual realization, or as the path itself.

Meanings: Intellectual leadership. Initiation. Secret knowledge. Religion. Churches, mosques, temples, meditation centers. Humility. Ritualism. Mercy. Compassion. Captivity to one's own ideas. Conformity. Rigid conservatism. A religious or spiritual leader. False guru. Hypocrisy. Hierarchy. Disbelief. Disillusionment. Knowledge that is not backed by experience.

THE LOVERS

VI The Lovers

A man and a woman kiss each other tenderly. Stars glimmer in their hair. The crown on the man's shirt shows that he feels like a king. The land around is vibrant with life; the water is a pool of love. Two birds are highlighted with a golden disk: love can give us wings. Lilies and red tulips grow near. A six-pointed star framing a yin-yang symbol is generated from the kiss.

The Cosmos The universe as perceived by the human mind comes forth from the interplay of opposites: male and female, light and dark, cold and hot, good and evil. Love unites opposites: in marriage, in reconciliation and forgiveness, in creation. The yin-yang symbol, with its round shape and the curved border between light and dark, shows the dynamic energy that ignites and unites opposites in the dance of the cosmos.

The Human Community All aspects of human society fluctuate over time. Technological innovation and conservation; communism and capitalism; conservatism and progressiveness; ethnocentricity and pluralism; hedonism and temperance are only a few of the opposing forces that flicker on and off, election by election, generation by generation.

The yin-yang sign shows that an opposing quality is inherent in each element: a dot of light in dark, a dot of dark in light. Conservatives in the United States favor a low profile for the government, and yet many feel that individual behavior, such as

27

sexual orientation and recreational drug use, should be regulated. Liberals oppose censorship, but find themselves in a quandary when free speech is used to support racism. People who are proud of immigrant roots may oppose open-door immigration policies.

The Lovers card can be seen as the harmonious society in which all differences are resolved and all opposites reconciled. More realistically, the Lovers is society as we know it, especially in places where differing points of view can be expressed freely—and must be accommodated. Like marriage, it has its ups and downs.

The Lovers can represent a time period in which a nation or group of people plunges into a crucible of change, a time in which the people will stand united or fall divided. It can also signify a treaty, alliance, or agreement between nations.

The Individual The image of the Lovers plays a role in all human life, whatever our lifestyle or orientation. It can torment us with the reminder of unrequited love, widowhood, or loneliness. It can inspire devotion in a lover, a husband or a wife, or in a celibate who yearns to unite with the divine. The urge for a partner, a mate, is often expressed as a wish for completion. A spouse is called "the other half," implying that wholeness is in the couple, not in each individual.

By itself, each element in a dualistic formula is incomplete. The Emperor is a cold, tyrannical father without the softening influence of the Empress; the Empress is an overindulgent mother without the discipline of the Emperor. We are often attracted to those who have traits we feel are lacking in ourselves. A mature love relationship, between friends or lovers, is one in which the partners are able to share each other's qualities, without expecting the relationship to solve all problems and fulfill every need.

The Lovers card is not a romantic fantasy. It is the readiness to love and be loved. It can indicate a lovable and loving person—the self or someone other.

Meanings: Union. Love. Blend of opposites. Tantra. Understanding of the cosmic dance. Harmony. Discernment. Decision. Beauty. Alliance. Treaties. Trust. Deep feeling. Optimism. Conflict between sacred and profane. Temptation. Doubts. Separation. A test or trial.

THE CHARIOT

VII The Chariot

Two horses pull a chariot in which a bearded man stands. The astrological symbol of Cancer is on the warrior's belt. A quiver of arrows and a bow are behind him. In the background is a castle.

The Cosmos Whereas the Lovers showed union or at least cohabitation of opposites, the Chariot shows a dynamic and tenuous duality. The horses, of opposite colors, do not blend as do the parts of the yin-yang symbol. They are bound, not united, in harness.

Change in nature is often a result of competition. The animal or plant that wins access to nutrition, habitat, and sexual partners will reproduce in the greatest numbers. Mutations that gain an edge in the survival game will end up as the norm, to be displaced by more change.

The Chariot is the force of change called evolution. It occurs over centuries or over days, step by inexorable step. Like natural evolution, the Chariot's path is both constructive and destructive. Some will survive; others will go extinct. The chariot driver may be headed toward a more viable situation, or he may take a wrong turn and dash into oblivion.

The Human Community Society, like the natural world, evolves under stress. Tensions among factions, classes, generations, and ethnic groups become too strong to be ignored or resolved. Revolutions, formations of new countries, decolonization, shifts of power right or left, as well as new suffrage laws, replacement of human labor by technology, and civil rights reforms are examples of social evolution.

The Chariot is unstoppable on its path. Social change can bring a feeling that, for better or worse, there is no turning back. Like changes in the natural ecosystem, every social change has reverberations that reach beyond the obvious.

The warrior driver of the Chariot is on a rough ride, and he must retain absolute control of the horses. Much can be accomplished through the harnessing of powers that oppose each other; confrontation can lead to constructive change. However, should the horses become implacable rivals, disaster will result. In human society, this is the win–lose, injury–retaliation mentality, with one side up and the other down—until the next upheaval—in a vicious cycle of power-grabbing that escalates into the calamity of war.

The image on the Chariot card can be seen as a tyrant (the driver) exercising power over his subjects (the horses). The most effective social motivation, though, comes from the people themselves. Ideally, the Chariot card is an integral image of a progressive society whose people are both driver and horses, in control and willing to work together for everyone's benefit.

The Individual The charioteer within a chariot is like the crab—symbol of Cancer—who rides within a shell. Armor, protection, security, and home are important to the person represented by the Chariot card. By extension, he has a keen sense of privacy, emotionally and physically.

The Chariot points to someone who is a survivor. Stick with this person during a shortage; his need for security, coupled with an awareness of the laws of supply and demand, means that he'll always have a stash to share. His relationships are governed by the same principles. He is most giving and most clinging, playing generosity against possessiveness.

The horses are black and white, indicating the interplay of physical and mental forces. Everyone faces, in important or trivial ways, what seems to be a battle between body and mind. Diets and alarm clocks are a few of the battlegrounds. Diseases such as arthritis, asthma, hypertension, digestive ailments, and even coronary disease, as well as mental conditions such as excessive guilt or scrupulousness, phobias, and compulsions are damage records of the war within ourselves.

The Chariot indicates the need to alternate the energies of body and mind, as well as the need to vary activities. Solitude should coexist with friendship. A bout of hard work should be followed by fun; after a long vacation or period of unemployment, work can be welcome.

Meanings: Adversity, possibly already overcome. Mental and physical balances. Conflicting influences. Hard work. Secure home. Resourcefulness. Obstacles. Turmoil. Vengeance. Hasty decision. Emotions nearly out of control. Failure. Last-minute losses. Sudden collapse of plans.

VIII Justice

The cloak of Justice spreads over the starry sky, in which are the yin-yang sign and a scale. On either side are day and night. A tower rises behind.

The Cosmos Libra, the sign of the zodiac whose sigil is at the base of the scale, begins at the autumn equinox, when day and night are of equal length. It is the time of year when the abundance of the living earth is celebrated in harvest; it is the time when many animals and plants bank down their life forces in preparation for winter.

The pictures of day and night symbolize the equilibrium of nature. Following the Lovers (Union) and the Chariot (Change), Justice shows the animate and inanimate forces of nature in equilibrium.

The Human Community The crucial factor in any justice system is the protection of individual rights without sacrifice of the society. Impartiality demands that the justice system see through bigotry, favoritism by class, the rigid status quo, legal loopholes, and security demands made by the state. The figure of Justice in the Cosmic Tarot is without the traditional blindfold. Her eyes are radiant with the ability to pierce darkness and reveal the truth.

Justice in the Cosmic Tarot lacks the traditional sword as well. True Justice is neither a cruel weapon used by the state to destroy opposition, nor a door to crime and anarchy. The tool of

Justice is a scale that rises from the divine rose of compassion, reflecting care for the defendant as well as for the prosecutor, and the balance of individual rights and social stability. The tower that illuminates her crown is a prison for evil-doers and a bulwark against human rights abuses.

Another facet of Justice, deriving from the rule of Libra, is diplomacy. Negotiations, peace talks, arbitration, ambassadors and embassies, and the United Nations are all in her care.

The Individual The pans of the scale of Justice weigh two red triangles. The upward-pointing triangle symbolizes intangible spirit; the downward-pointing triangle symbolizes the body and all matter that keeps us (as incarnate beings) attached to earthly existence. Each red triangle is invested with a black triangle, as each half of the yin-yang circle is invested with its opposite.

The image describes our individuality, which is generated by a dualistic outlook of "me" and "you," and our unity with what is all around us. Selfishness and compassion are implicit. The pans are in perfect equilibrium. A rose, symbol of physical passion and divine love, supports the scale. The dualism and unity of Justice illustrates the inner person and also the individual relating to others.

Libra, the sign of the scales, is ruled by the planet of love, Venus, and so is considered one of the more sociable signs of the zodiac. Charm, good looks, diplomacy, and affability are considered Libran qualities; romance, courtship, and romantic intrigue are favored activities.

The wish for equilibrium is foremost. Libras judge, weigh, and evaluate. Indecision or vacillation may result from the wish to consider all sides of a story. Justice can indicate a decision—or more procrastination. When the verdict is finally delivered, it will be fair. The process may be unfathomable, especially to the party who feels cheated of a favorable outcome.

The Cosmic Tarot

Meanings: Reasonableness. Justice through knowledge of a higher order. Balance. Harmony. Equity. Diplomacy. Arbitration. Union of opposites. Righteousness. Virtue. Honor. Kindness. Charm. Attractive person. Just reward. Dignity. Equilibrium. Poise. Impartiality. Bias. False accusations. Prejudice. Severity. Intolerance. Unfairness.

THE HERMIT

IX The Hermit

A man with flowing hair and beard is in yoga posture under a flowering tree. On his scarf is the symbol of Jupiter, the planet ruling philosophy, the symbol of the sun, light of knowledge, and the symbol of the astrological sign Virgo. The moon rises and a star drops light to where another star lies hidden by the mountains. A lamp sheds starry light at the Hermit's feet. A pink flower glows and a night bird looks on.

The Cosmos The Sanskrit letter on the headband of the Hermit spells OM, the most powerful and mysterious mantra of Hindus and Buddhists. OM has no semantic meaning. It is the pure sound that vibrates between the material world and the spirit. It is nothing and everything. The person who chants the mantra imbues it with significance through meditation, study, and devotion. OM expresses in sound the oneness of the universe.

The Human Community The reclusive Hermit is not part of the world at large. He is the individual teachers encountered in life. His influence on society is made indirectly, through his students. Inevitably, the Hermit's teachings will be institutionalized by his followers as a church, an academic institution, or a government. At that point, they are something altogether different from the teachings received directly from the Hermit, as different as the Hermit is from the Hierophant. The Hermit himself stays the same, whatever riches or prestige come his way. He is real—not a charlatan or an ego-tripper.

The lamp shines with the teachings that the Hermit has received in his turn. Without teachers—gurus, ministers, parents, siblings, school teachers, elder or younger friends—humans have no means to follow the way of truth. The Hermit represents the flow of ethics, wisdom, and knowledge from one person to another, and from generation to generation. He is both student and teacher.

The Individual The Hermit is a solitary, studious, disciplined person. He is reserved and has a somber demeanor, possibly serene or possibly severe. He may live alone, though his integrity does not hinge on solitude. The Hermit can be eclectic to the point of eccentricity, or he can be fanatically single-minded. His nature is firm, though not rigid. He remains true to his path, unswayed by the fortunes of life, unimpressed by his own accomplishments. He considers everything a gift from his teachers.

The scarf over the Hermit's left arm has on it the sigil of Virgo. The Virgin, who rules the sign of Virgo with the planet Mercury, symbolizes chastity, and conservation together with abundance. Libra follows Virgo in the zodiac and weighs the gathered harvest; in Virgo, the corn is still on the stalk, the wheat in the ear. All is ripe and yet unexploited. The solitary Hermit conserves the energies of his body as fuel for his spiritual journey. He teaches us prudence with material resources and with our bodies and minds.

The Cosmic Tarot

The Hermit can indicate a fruitful period of study, meditation, and contemplation, or a change to a more quiet lifestyle. In a negative sense, the Hermit may warn of alienation, withdrawal from other people, depression, emotional numbness, even paranoia.

Meanings: Seclusion. Wisdom. Discernment. Cleverness. Self-control. Awareness. Autonomy. Reliability. Discipline. Knowledge. Solitude. Prudence. Discretion. Withdrawal. Regression. Annulment. Chastity. Conservation. Alienation. Loneliness. Imprudence. Prematurity. Dullness. Impotence.

WHEEL OF FORTUNE

X Wheel of Fortune

A network of circles, squares, and triangles turns in the cosmos. The symbolic design resembles clockworks. The Wheel of Fortune is one of three cards in the Major Arcana that does not show a human figure. (The other two are Death and The Moon.) Hence, the Wheel does not generally point to a person or type of person.

The Cosmos The magical mechanism of our solar system is diagrammed in the Wheel of Fortune. The center holds the sun, from which radiate like petals of a flower the cosmic bodies known to the ancients: (from top clockwise) Saturn, Jupiter, Venus, Moon, Mercury, and Mars. (Neptune, Uranus, and Pluto are not included, as they were not discovered until modern times.) Next comes the zodiac: (from left counterclockwise) Aries, Taurus, Gemini, Cancer, Leo, Virgo,

Libra, Scorpio, Sagittarius, Capricorn, Aquarius, and Pisces. At the top immediately outside the zodiac are Neptune and Uranus, and above these, in the center, is Pluto. The four corners hold the four elements: (from left top, clockwise) water, air, earth, and fire. The bottom central orb is a symbol of the unity of the four elements, and also of the planet Earth.

Together, the yellow orbs of the planets form the diagram of the Cabalistic Tree of Life. The Hebrew word near Pluto, at the top, reads Kether, which is the head of the Tree of Life. Kether is the Crown of Creation, which can be considered as the inspiration of an unknowable, unnameable godhead. The Hebrew word at the bottom is Malkuth, the Kingdom of Earth, by which is meant not the element of earth or the planet, but the terrestrial experience, the physical universe, generally from the point of view of humankind.

The Cabala, a system of esoteric teachings rooted in Judaism, is a beautiful and glorious study, whether one is Jewish, Muslim, or Christian, or even if one follows an Eastern path. It illuminates any religion or philosophy, as well as exalting our intellect, emotions, and senses. In a sense, the Cabala is like the tantric systems of Hinduism and Buddhism, and a trustworthy teacher is the first thing a would-be student should seek. Common wisdom has it that the immature or solitary student can go mad from studying the Cabala too deeply. Like tantra, the study does have a safeguard: its real secrets can be passed on only by direct transmission—living teacher to living student. The name "Cabala," after all, is from Hebrew word qabal, "to receive."

The Tree of Life pictured on the Wheel of Fortune expresses symbolically the inspiration of the ineffable "One Mind" or "God's thought" moving through different modes of potential (emanations) and finally manifesting in the diversity of material being. This operation is both pollution and exaltation. Flesh binds the spirit, the spirit inspires the flesh. It is through movement on the Tree, not through stasis, that we express our divine humanity.

The Cosmic Tarot

The Tree is a scheme, a ladder, as it were, that can help human faculties connect with God.

The Human Community For centuries, the Wheel of Fortune was illustrated with a medieval image. A wheel to which are bound four kings is turned by the blindfolded goddess of fortune. The king at the top of the wheel blithely says, "I reign." The king at the bottom bears the wheel on his back and says, "I am without reign." One king ascends hopefully: "I will reign." Another king descends: "I have reigned."

The Age of Reason took a less fatalistic view of government. Humanity would evolve over time a society of justice, love, and material abundance. The United States was formed partly on such an ideal. This utopia is a variation on the medieval Christian City of God, with trust moved from God to the (God-given) human qualities of reason and compassion.

The medieval Wheel of Fortune seems to deny that humankind has any control over its destiny. It dictates that the rise and fall of nations is an inexorable cycle to which all are help-lessly bound.

We are indeed bound by circumstances of history and nature, but men and women possess the means to better soci-ety. Utopian visions can nurture the quest, even if lack of insight of ourselves and the world around us provides a sense that the blind goddess rules our fortunes. Social evolution is a trial and error process; we must learn from our triumphs and from our errors.

The Individual The Wheel of Fortune can indicate an ecstatic experience of oneness with the universe, and a break-through in understanding natural law. Spiritual life is integrated with worldly activities. Realization of the impermanent nature of things can bring comfort, or it can cause great sadness. As well, the Wheel can indicate a healing of body and mind. One can feel that one is again "behind the wheel," in control. Conversely, the

Wheel may show stagnation, which can take the form of "bad luck" or a sense of being manipulated by circumstances.

Meanings: Realization of the cosmic order. Application of higher laws. Dance of energies. Healing. Constant changes. Fortune. Turning point. "As above, so below." Good or bad luck, depending on other influences. Inevitability. Lack of control.

STRENGTH

XI Strength

A woman holds a magic cloth that mirrors a lion. The sun is at her crown. The lush, brilliant landscape is threatened by a smoldering volcano.

The Cosmos The trident and the white stripes on the lion's head indicate devotion to Shiva. The Hindu god Shiva personifies destruction and reproduction, part of the trinity of Brahma the creator and Vishnu the preserver. The object commonly worshiped as embodying Shiva is the lingam, which represents Shiva's energy as well as his ultimate formlessness.

Strength is energy that is available, without discrimination or judgment, to creative as well as annihilating forces. The woman's forehead is marked with lines that denote devotion to Vishnu the Preserver. Maintaining is another form of strength.

The Human Community The image of a naked woman whose only "defense" is a cloth on which a lion is pictured reveals one of the basic paradoxes maintained by governments:

the idea that a show of strength—a standing army and large arsenals—is necessary to maintain peace. Complete disarmament is to most people the international equivalent of no police. Few are willing to place such trust in our world.

The extreme show of strength is armed-to-the-teeth nationalism and an iron police force. Fascism in pre-World War II Europe presented a seductive sense of security amidst the economic woes following World War I and the chaotic transition from monarchy to democracy or communism.

Economic and historic/cultural pressures repeatedly draw people all over the world to fascism. Inevitably, the strength extolled by fascists is revealed as brutality: the dictator's boot which was to crush the "enemy" crushes the citizens, the invigorating rhetoric of nationalism turns out to be a balloon filled with poison gas.

Armies and police must be flexible and fully accountable to the people. The infallible test of a strong government is its ability to maintain human rights for all citizens when difficult conditions arise. The woman and the lion represent intelligent compassion clothed with power.

The card Strength directs attention to the armed forces and the police, and their degree of strength or weakness.

The Individual Shiva embraces the energy of the body, or shakti, represented as a coiled snake, kundalini. The science of kundalini yoga is complex, but on one level it involves awakening the natural energy of the body in order to exalt the mind. Like Cabalistic studies, kundalini yoga should not be undertaken casually. The smoldering volcano on the Strength card is a hint of the destructive power that can be let loose in the body and psyche of a careless or unprepared student. It is a serious mistake to try to teach oneself kundalini yoga, or to place oneself in the hands of an unqualified or unethical teacher.

The lily at the left of the woman, and her nudity, indicate that inner purity—unselfishness—is a way of preparing for the rising of the snake of kundalini. The bright light of the sun behind the woman's head and the rearing snake of her headdress indicate that the woman's energy is flowing freely.

Strength allows feats of physical strength, and it fosters will and charisma. One might be getting in touch with deeper powers, including one's own femininity or masculinity, and this can be a source of great joy and of sudden, unexpected popularity. A meeting with a person who is both mysterious and magnetic can take place. Taken too far, the energy can lead to over-indulgence or a hunger for power over others. If the energy hints of going out of control, the best thing to do is withdraw and rest until equilibrium is fully regained.

Strength brings determination to recover from mental illness (especially phobias, anxiety, or obsessiveness) or physical illness (especially lingering or chronic conditions and cardiovascular disease). It is the ability and the sincere desire to free oneself of addiction: the opportunity is always here. A support group is a form of Strength, in itself and in the courage of the person who admits that he or she needs help.

Strength is, of course, the companion to athletes and exercisers on all levels. The marathon runner and the wheelchair roller, the "minnow" child who just joined the swim team and the elder who swims to strengthen an arthritic body can enjoy this card. Strength calls on everyone of all abilities to participate in the joy of physical activity.

Strength also reflects the joy we take in sharing the world with animals, domestic and wild.

Meanings: Energy. Enjoying the dance of life. Creative energy. Wildness. Determination to live. Strength. Courage. Conviction. Resolution. Recovery. Confidence. Zeal. Mind over matter. Vice. Weakness. Lack of faith. Powerlessness.

THE HANGED MAN

XII The Hanged Man

In most tarot decks, the Hanged Man is suspended by a noose. The Cosmic Tarot depicts a youth who hangs as if by magic, or great strength, from the branch of a leafy tree. His hands are folded in prayer, and the moon forms a halo around his head. The perspective of the picture gives the impression that he is floating in the sky; his hair reaches toward earth, but doesn't quite touch. Look at the card upside down, and the sky resembles an ocean with whitecaps receding into the distance.

The Cosmos If the Fool is "spirit on the edge of manifestation, the formless who precedes or succeeds the dualism of heaven and earth," the Hanged Man is Spirit amidst manifestation, and he dwells between heaven and earth. He is the Fool after the leap from the precipice—long after the leap, after whole universes have come into being. The Fool is poised between destruction and creation, with no bias or inclination toward either. The Hanged Man dangles between creation and destruction, but because he has been "corrupted" by matter, the implication is that of movement toward destruction, death, or annihilation. In other words, the Hanged Man is spirit bound by time and place.

The Human Community Once in a while someone comes along and turns the world upside down. Political economist Karl Marx, American patriot Thomas Jefferson, the Jodo

42

Shinshu (True Pure Land Buddhist) sage Shinran, artist Andy Warhol, Saint Francis of Assisi, founder of Christian Science Mary Baker Eddy, civil rights leader Martin Luther King, and the radical feminist, self-named "Revolting Hag" Mary Daly are a few of those who, like it or not, forced us to look at our lives and our society in a totally new way.

We glorify these diverse men and women, and we crucify them: often we martyr them into sainthood. King was assassinated, Shinran exiled from his own land. Some have thrived, in spite of fierce opposition and even ridicule. Their names may be unfamiliar to many, but whether they act politically, artistically, or religiously, as individuals or as groups, these extraordinary minds motivate the transitions of human society.

The Individual Why would a young man choose such a deliberately uncomfortable position for his prayers? Anyone who has attempted any kind of spiritual work, within or outside of religious tradition, very soon finds that it is uncomfortable. Kneeling or sitting in meditation, fasting, breaking out of worldly routines—all of these devices remove us from our everyday lives.

As children, we changed our perspective by spinning round and round until we were dizzy-drunk, or by hanging upside down from a bar at the playground. Upside down, the world is comic and grotesque, or exotic and beautiful. Features that were unnoticed can loom large.

As adults, we may use film, television, books, or drugs to escape from our lives. Unfortunately, grownups very quickly become habituated to these activities and are once again locked into the mundaneness being evaded. So, we up the dose, look for something new, or settle down into a numb routine.

Religious practice can fall into the same syndrome: the enthusiasm of the convert, the frustration of the novice, the boredom of the senior. Those who last, endure the ups and downs with equanimity. Insight and the support of friends and teachers are encouraging. Many people favor occasional retreats, with or without others, as a way to refresh the spirit.

The Hanged Man dangles all alone between earth and sky. His teacher has brought him this far; now it is time to go alone. He has temporarily renounced worldly life in favor of prayer and meditation. His face is tranquil, though he has been ravaged by terror at the death of self-driven activity, depression at the loss of earthly attachments, elation at being without the weight of daily life, as well as vertigo brought by such weightlessness, horror in the face of unending loneliness, and bliss in undisturbed solitude. He observes and accepts the flow of emotions with equilibrium; his tranquil concentration is unwavering.

The Hanged Man's support, the tree, grows from the earth, and it enables him to plant his foot in the sky. The dense physical and emotional qualities of earth and the transcending, "empty" qualities of the sky are calmly united in his practice.

Meanings: Overcoming obstacles through devotion. Peace of mind. Prudence. Insight. Life in suspension. Transition. Change. Abandonment. Renunciation. The changing of life's forces. A still point between dramatic events. Sacrifice. The approach of new life forces. Unwillingness to make any effort or to give of oneself. Ego-tripping. False prophecy. Useless sacrifice. Playing martyr to manipulate others.

XIII Death

A skeleton on a stone plain holds a scythe and a blackbird. Behind him the sun hovers over an ocean, its light contained by a square. Beyond is the endless cosmos.

The skulls, the stopped clock, and the broken jewels and sword symbolize the limits of human life. Even the tombstone itself, the final house of the body and symbol of remembrance, falls into ruins. The ocean is a metaphor of existence, whether existence is seen as a life span bounded by birth and death, or as the cycle of reincarnation in which birth and death are alternating pulsations.

The Cosmos Hindu cosmology sees the birth and extinction of universes as the exhalation and inhalation of the breath of god, an ongoing cycle of existential suffering that one can escape only as a "twice-born" individual. Christian and Islamic beliefs posit individual salvation (or damnation) that is realized after death, as well as a collective City of God, or Earthly Paradise, in which the entire world is purged of heretics and infidels and then glorified in worship of the "true" god. All of these systems have in common an apocalypse: an era of evil, suffering, fear, moral corruption, and finally destruction. Humankind seems to feel that the present world must die in order for a heavenly world to be born.

The skeleton stands like a gateway between physical existence and the naked universal soul or mind: consciousness without the trappings and distractions of flesh, the metaphysical

The Cosmic Tarot

City of God, maybe even Paradise, a realm that perfects life as we know it. Or the skeleton can be simply a hollow boneman, mocking our aspirations with an image of extinction and nothingness: a dead-end apocalypse, ultimate mortality. The sun could be rising, or it could be setting.

The Human Community Society progresses with the death of human generations, as well as with the death of technologies, countries, and ideologies. Mahatma Gandhi, speaking of the struggle of India for independence from Britain, equated death with purification through suffering: "No country has ever risen without being purified through the fire of suffering. The mother suffers so that her child may live. The condition of wheat-growing is that the seed grain should perish. Life comes out of death. Will India rise out of her slavery without fulfilling this eternal law of purification through suffering?"

"Death" sometimes comes as a dramatic upheaval—coups d'etat, the rise or fall of dictatorships or democracies, assassinations, wars, displacement of workers by machines or corporate restructuring—or as a smooth change, as when an entrenched party is voted out of office or a business passes to a new generation.

A society that does not change, stagnates. Continuity and traditions that have served generations well must not obstruct regeneration and innovation.

The Individual Rare is the person who can honestly claim no fear of death. At some point, however, everyone must recognize the inevitability of death, hopefully before being forced by the event itself. Though it is extremely painful, to say the least, to contemplate separation from our loved ones and the loss of our body, talents, and possessions, an honest encounter with death can give purpose to life. We have a limited amount of time to fulfill ourselves and to help others to find happiness.

The Death card does not predict that a death will soon occur—Death does not come at the behest of a tarot card. It does remind us not to put off what we want to do with our lives, since all of us will die sooner or later. If we feel that our salvation lies in religion, we should build a practice now, rather than waiting until we're sick or senile and less capable of training mind and body. If we feel that we want to leave something beautiful behind, we should begin our creation today. If we love someone, we should express it. If we have an enemy, we should work on being reconciled, at least in our hearts, if not openly. If life discontents us, we may be taking for granted the precious joys embedded in mundane existence.

The boneman with the sickle is also known as Father Time. The Death card can indicate change, transition, and the passage of time. Sorrow or joy at the end of a phase may be indicated. Both the let-down and the relief at finishing a long work, whose reception in the world is yet uncertain, might be felt. A move to another home is possible, with painful detachment from the present place mixed with pleasurable anticipation of what the future home may bring.

Meanings: The end. Transition. A boundary reached. Transformation. Passage of time. Clearing away the old to make way for the new. Determination to "turn over a new leaf." Unexpected change. Loss. A familiar situation or friendship ends. Stagnation. Separation. Immobility. Inertia. Taxes.

XIV Temperance

A beautiful woman pours water from two cups into a fresh stream bordered by irises. A heron is behind the woman. The sun, though half-hidden by clouds, blazes strongly.

The Cosmos   The Chariot demonstrated dynamic change whose energy derived from tension and competition. Temperance is change through the blending of elements, gradually and naturally. The seasons, day and night, the mighty yet aeonian migration of earth's continents, the shift of the earth's axis of rotation which changes the zodiac, even the drops of water that over years can wear away a rock—all are in the realm of Temperance. Dramatic and violent events—earthquakes, volcanos, floods, typhoons—are not directly in her rule.

Temperance is the force of transformation. She is the universal comfort, the life-line between extinction and rebirth. As the water flows from the cups into the stream, and gradually moves to the sea, so after death our psyches and physical forms are transformed, and possibly liberated, in ways we cannot imagine.

The Human Community   The woman returns the waters to the stream, and in doing so practices one of the cardinal rules of maintaining balance in any system: return in some way what has been taken. She is partly nude, but not completely nature's child—she wears rich jewels; her foot dips into the stream and yet is shod. The land that stretches behind her is semi-cultivated.

Temperance focuses on social stability in terms of resources and economy. Though many scholars admit to apparently random, unpredictable elements in a nation's economy, one "rule" is evident: "What goes up, must come down." If stocks soar, get ready for a crash. If a nation is pumped up with loans, it will be deflated with debt. Extremes beget extremes.

The same applies to natural resources. We have the technology and the understanding necessary for enjoying nature's riches without pollution. Greed destroys the balance.

Temperance can be understood as a balanced budget, sound environmental policies, and/or a healthy economy in which the distribution of wealth is equitable. Alternatively, it can reflect the ebb and flow in the fortunes of nations and peoples.

The Individual   Around 600 B.C., a young prince left his father's palace and a life of luxury in order to find the ultimate truth as to the nature of life. Fleeing to a forest, he stripped off his riches and practiced austerities. His bones rose to his skin, but he did not attain his goal. Too late, he realized that luxury and asceticism were both extremes that would not bring him closer to the truth. Starvation had brought him only the imminence of death: "Mine eyes are dim now that they need to see the truth." (From *The Light of Asia,* by Edwin Arnold.) But a housewife, thinking him a nature god, revived him with an offering of milk and rice. Strengthened, the seeker was able to withstand the final onslaught of the selfish ego, and he became enlightened. From thenceforth he was called the Buddha, the Awakened One.

Most people, especially in developed countries, would consider the lives of Buddhist monks more austere than moderate. However, ordinary people can try to find a way of living that creates the least possible harm and disturbance to others, while allowing individual balance and expression.

Temperance has become a rather distasteful virtue. Popular

culture glamorizes emotional upheavals, violence, and passion. A temperate individual is often portrayed as a dried-up prude or as an ax-wielding Carry Nation figure—but these characters are also extremes.

The temperate man or woman does not have to be an intolerant wet-blanket, a boor or bored, or a celibate teetotaler. Temperance is not the bland repression of joy, sorrow, sexual feelings, and so on. It involves acceptance of our feelings rather than rejection or selection of them: the rough with the smooth.

Temperance can be the fruit of a hard, honest look at one's life. Are we draining our energy chasing thrills, while continuing to suffer the same problems over and over? Are we exploiting or walking over other people in the quest for more riches and new highs?

Temperance is a realistic way of living unselfishly. We learn truly to enjoy life. In Temperance, we may experience more subtle levels of joy and understanding.

Meanings: Mental equilibrium. The middle way. Improvement. Rejuvenation. Moderation. Temperance. Patience. Accommodation. Bringing people together. A matchmaker. Management. Fusion. Inability to work with others. Carelessness.

XV The Devil

THE DEVIL

A creature part man and part beast poses before a prison, surrounded by the victims of his reign. A man on his right seems unaware of his chains as he tries to stride away. A woman is chained within the walls of a prison. At the Devil's left hand, another woman stands on the back of a man. She enjoys her dominance, but she, too, is in chains; those who oppress others are oppressed, though they often fail to see this.

The Cosmos The Lovers card showed the union of opposites through love; the Devil presents what opposes union. In emotional terms, it is hatred; in metaphysical terms, it is ignorance. Here is the existence that our "New Age" does not acknowledge, though whether New-Aged or old-aged, we continue to exist and suffer in it. The Devil offers no true marriage, no union, no creation.

Ironically, primeval ignorance is expressed in the Hebrew Scriptures (Old Testament) as the knowledge of good and evil. This "knowledge" is not to be confused with the conscience, which occasionally prevents us from acting on hatred and anger, or encourages us to act in wisdom.

The knowledge that the Devil offers is the conviction that we have a self separate from and opposed to others. Adam's and Eve's self-consciousness was manifest in their wish to clothe their natural bodies, to hide from God. As long as we hold the conviction of self, we are ignorant of blissful union.

The Devil separates being from being, creation from creator.

The Cosmic Tarot

While this may seem a problem for the individual to work out, it is an essential component in the unending cosmic cycle of suffering to which all beings are subject, a world in which nature decrees that we—humans, cats, dogs, insects, birds, fish, plants, microorganisms—must kill each other in order to survive.

The Human Community   The Devil emerges from a deteriorating structure and is himself in a state of deterioration. His hold on his disciples remains untarnished; the chains are the shiniest part of the image. His horns recall animalistic energy, but the ring through his nose recalls the servitude and bondage of animals such as farm oxen. His costume mixes church and military dress, reflecting the age-old problem of the corruption of religion by power. The "church" is not necessarily religion as commonly understood. A political ideology can substitute for religion.

Torture, unjust detention, "disappearances," and death penalty (execution) are the evil reflections of a defective social system. When state power is threatened by protest or rebellion, the repression intensifies. War does not represent the pitting of one unified society against another unified society, although propaganda says otherwise. History shows that war breaks out when the conflicting elements within a nation are projected onto an "enemy." Charismatic individuals who exploit hatred, fear, and ignorance bedevil the world.

The Devil crumbles, but the chains are renewed. Society must use caution in creating its prison and military and police structures; they easily assume much power and are not easily cast off. Active human rights advocates can ensure that institutions of abuse are more and more difficult to hide from the rest of the world.

The Individual   People often try to gain their wishes by manipulating others. Methods range from tears to fists, from threats of abandonment and financial deprivation to wax voodoo dolls. The first step to freedom for one who is in the role of "victim" is to face the problem and the fact that it can't be wished or hoped away. Then, one must seek help, over and over again, until one has the strength and resources to break away.

The inverted star on the Devil's necklace indicates still another form of repression: capitulation to materialism and pleasure. The five senses, represented by the five points of the star, point earthward; the body is enslaved to the getting of riches and rich sensations. Such a density of earth element, the senses cleaving to material earth, is decadence, as when an animal falls to the ground and decays. Exploitation, prostitution, bondage, slavery, perversion: anything becomes possible.

The Devil represents the lowest point in the cycle of life. At the bottom, however, there is hope: the only way to go is up. Recovery is a struggle that few can make alone. Now is the time to find supportive friends and guides, reliable people who will not exploit the situation and set the cycle in motion once more. More often than not, we emerge from our life struggles with new strength and wisdom, and compassion for others who are where we were.

Meanings: Victory of materialism. Occult powers. Slavery. Dependence. Perversion. Subordination. Ravage. Bondage. Passion. Egoism. Malevolence. Subservience. Weird experience. Bad outside influence or advice. Black magic. Unexpected failure. Violence. Self-punishment. Temptation to evil. Overcoming one's fears. Perception of the inner demon. Throwing off shackles. Divorce. Recognition of one's needs by another person. Overcoming severe handicaps. The beginning of spiritual understanding.

THE TOWER

XVI The Tower

The eye of God blasts a tower. Fire engulfs the top stories, and two people and a crown fall. Pride has lifted the Tower to reach for the heavens.

The Cosmos However intriguing cosmologies may be, however intellectually stimulating, in the end they are only systems of human thought. All of the religions and philosophies of earth cannot really touch the heavens; they can only try to point the way. One can consider the image on the Tower card as divine awareness, the eye of God, turning its searing ray on the edifice of human cosmology. The pride invested in the cleverness of it all tumbles down as easily as the fancy crown falls to the depths. Pure experience, clear awareness, cannot be replaced by intellectualization.

The Human Community The Tower recalls the Hebrew Scriptures (Old Testament) story of the Tower of Babel (Genesis 11). The people attempted to make a tower to reach the heavens. To stop them, God scattered them about the earth and their common tongue was splintered into diverse languages. The partially built tower was abandoned.

The pious rejoice in the justness of God's sentence on upstart humankind. A nagging question remains, though. Wasn't the work to reach the heavens a noble one? And who can help but mourn the shattering of a primeval understanding among humankind, an understanding so perfect it seemed to threaten

God himself. The tumbling crown on XVI The Tower offers a clue to one way of interpreting the story.

The crown is a symbol of earthly power. Who wears the crown rules earth. In medieval times, the anointed royalty felt themselves to be closer to God than the commoners. Richard I, called the Lionheart, claimed that the only one who outranked him was God himself. Partly his words were defiance to the Papacy, but a feeling of innate superiority conditioned him and his fellow royalty. The brutal exploitation of peasants by the ruling class showed no human sympathy.

In the same way, slave holders and colonialists all over the world persuaded themselves that their race or nationality and their technology and material condition gave them the right, indeed the obligation, to dominate and "guide" people of other lands and races. Colonialism, racist "supremacy," sexism, and classism are all manifestations of conceit on a social scale.

Ultimately, the most powerful and the most abject are equal in spirit. A tower of brick is basically a pile of mud. Attempts to reach heaven through material structures and human-directed projects throw us right back on the ground.

The Individual   The Tower is a symbol of the status quo, entrenched ways of thinking and living. Carefully built security in lifestyle and dogma walls off inspiration and spontaneity. Snobbishness and arrogance block any insight one might have of oneself or others.

Opening up can be painful, a real trauma. The lightning of exposure can take the form of an uncomfortable glimpse into our own complacency, or it can be a shattering, life-transforming event. The Tower can represent an unpleasant person, one who forces us to deal with the negative aspects of our own personalities.

Meanings: Forced change. Breakdown. Ruin. Fight. Catastrophe. Destruction. Break up of constricting convictions. Arrogance. An unpleasant and unwelcome person. An intrusion on a complacent existence. Intolerance. Disappointment. Chance for a new start. Liberation. Enthusiasm. Complete and sudden change. Continued oppression. Living in a rut. Inability to change.

THE STAR

XVII The Star

A woman stands on the edge of a lake, a flamingo at her side. She pours water from two cups into the lake, the liquid pouring over a lotus. The rays of the star in the sky meet the moon, the star on the woman's headband, and a rising star.

The Cosmos The six-pointed Magen David (Star of David) is a symbol of the ancient religion of Judaism. The Hebrew people evolved a monotheistic religion in the midst of a pagan land. Like the Brahma-Vishnu-Shiva triad which is in reality one godhead, Yahweh (Jehovah), who is called Adonai, is creator-sustainer-destroyer all in one.

The six-pointed star shows two triangles, one pointing up and one pointing down. These triangles can be seen to represent the action of the animal or earthly body aspiring to spirit, and the spirit becoming incarnate, inhabiting the body. In the book of Genesis, man is earth-dust vivified by the breath of the divine creator; the word "spirit" derives from Latin spiritus, breath. In the same way, the Egyptian creator Ptah fashioned clay statues of humans and breathed life into them. Jesus is called the Word (of God) made flesh, and the Word rides on the breath (hence, the power of praying or chanting aloud). Many Hindus consider

Christ to be like Krishna, an avatar (emanation) of Vishnu, the deity descended into bodily form.

We are all like Christ or Krishna; we all contain the breath of divine potency in the earthen vessel of our flesh. The beautiful woman on the Star represents divinity in nature.

The Human Community The Star is the ecology card of the tarot. Unashamed of her natural body, unafraid to stir the waters of the deep, the woman circulates the waters, as the rain feeds the waterfall, as ground water feeds the spring that wells up from below. The bird at the woman's side is trusting.

Humankind will never return en masse to the primitive life, unless a grand catastrophe wipes out civilization. However, we vitally need to stay in touch with our earth. Nature is a mirror of society and of humankind's collective consciousness, or soul, or karma. Exploitation or generosity, carelessness or long-term planning, ignorance or knowledge: all are reflected in the rivers, the mountains, the oceans, the sky.

The Individual The Star is one of the most auspicious cards in the deck. It is pure hope, unstained by arrogance, disappointment, and doubt, hope before the solidifying act of faith, fluid and inspired. The hope of the Star is not grounded in material or psychological desire; it is the thought of salvation or enlightenment, hope for the good of all beings. The Star illuminates the divinity in everyone and everything; it is the realm of miracles.

The experience of the Star can be one of those days when you wake up joyous for no special reason, a day when the faces of people on the street are beautiful even with the suffering that marks them. The experience of the Star can be divine ecstasy.

Meanings: Hope. Beauty. Brilliance. Clarity. Inspiration. Unconventional person. Bright prospects. Mixing of the past and present. Optimism. Return of childhood faith brings joy amidst sorrow. Something valuable which one thought lost is found. Insight. Astrological influence. Fantasies. Resignation.

THE MOON

XVIII The Moon

A crayfish crawls out of the waters, attracted by the moon. Within the moon are two fish, symbolic of the astrological sign Pisces, which is ruled by watery Neptune. The sky opens to the immensity of the cosmos.

The Cosmos A metaphor of the way in which lunar forces manifest can be seen in the tides of the earth. We cannot see any force emanating from the moon to perform the massive work of moving earth's oceans, rivers, lakes, and topsoil. The unseen, intangible force of the moon is perceived only through its effects.

The Human Community Archetypically, the moon rules the unconscious, the part of the mind that is unknown to us, and yet can motivate our actions and thoughts. The unconscious is not evil in itself, but it is dangerous in that it can circumvent reason and conscience, and powerful in that its roots lie partly in physical and emotional gratification.

In *The Undiscovered Self*, Carl Jung points to the danger of a society in which reason and insight do not figure strongly. Fanatic, fantasizing types know how to fish in the depths of the collective unconscious to draw forth psychotic behavior from the masses: genocide, witch hunts, totalitarianism, cruel excesses in scientific research on animals and humans, citizens spying on citizens, "ethnic cleansing."

Two questions arise after atrocities are made unbearably clear to the world. When did we realize what was happening—and why did we let it continue? We fear the answer to such questions.

Facing up to the obscure currents of human nature need not be an exercise in pessimism or self-flagellation. Manifestations of social insanity are easily recognizable: cruelty and prejudice are the major distinguishing characteristics. Like any serious illness, they should not be ignored—especially since they tend to run a plague course if unchecked. Self-knowledge is at least a beginning of responsibility for our actions.

The moon has a bright face as well as an obscure one. Inspiration arises from the depths of the psyche to find expression in the arts, which in turn illuminate the human psyche through engaging all our faculties: the senses, the intellect, the emotions, the imagination. An art work can be polemic or propagandistic, but the most effective are not those that have the answers, but those that raise questions, stimulating insight. Solidarity and sympathy among people can come simply through exposition of the human heart. When an Asian is moved by an African dance, when a Tennessee Williams play meets with great success in Russia, we find that we are not so different from each other after all.

The moon rules healing that depends on intuition and faith, rather than empirical science and technology. Many of us have had the experience of visiting doctor after doctor, until we finally connect with one who makes the proper diagnosis and prescribes a helpful treatment. Healers with lunar power can be found in mainstream medicine, but tend to gravitate to alternative and folk medicine, especially herbalism.

The Individual   Like the moon, Pisces is able to see into the darkness. Emotional life, the hidden currents of the psyche, clairvoyance, inexplicable urges: all are to Pisces as water to the fish. Though Pisces is able to absorb and reflect the emotions of others, he or she is introverted, inclined to hide his or her own deeper feelings.

Pisces might be a mystic, a teacher, a speculative scientist, an artist—especially an actor; or Pisces can descend into delusions of power with witchery, charlatanism, a "celebrity complex," or even fascism. The forces of the moon act strongly on the watery temperament of Pisces, evoking vulnerability, susceptibility, and the tendency to indulge in languid pleasures and mind-altering substances. Like a fish, Pisces will submerge himself or herself in the element chosen, easily becoming an egotistical socialite, an addict of drugs and/or dreams, a fanatic; or a charismatic leader, a martyr who sacrifices everything for his or her faith, a true medium, a devoted and sensitive lover, a great actor who enlightens us with his or her portrayal of the undercurrents of human life.

The individual symbolized by the Moon can be one who is "all things to all people." We gravitate to these celebrities, all vulnerability and all charisma, with great talent often inextricably mixed with an androgynous persona.

"Lunar" qualities have been called "feminine," in contrast to the "solar, masculine" qualities. Women are perceived to be more at home in the realm of the emotions and are supposed to be more intuitive. In fact, beyond the amount of emotional display allowed by culture, men seem to feel as much joy, sorrow, anger, and so on, as women, and women have all the rational and analytical faculties that men have. The bisection and segregation of the human psyche into so-called masculine and feminine elements is absurd.

The Moon warns of hidden currents, possibly gossip and intrigue. The Moon can also indicate a breakthrough, especially in scholarly or artistic work. With sudden insight, a new realm opens.

The twelve stars around the moon are arranged like the hours of a clock, indicating time perceived as a cycle, rather than as linear.

For women of child-bearing age, the Moon directs attention to reproductive health, as the menstrual cycle generally synchronizes with the moon's cycle. The Moon may indicate thoughts about having children. The Moon can also signal menopause.

Meanings: Salvation. Mercy. Emotions. Sensitivity. Artistic talent. The unconscious. Hidden mental power. To forget oneself. Drugs. Dreams. Extrasensory perception. Intuition. Secrets revealed. Intrigue. Gossip.

XIX The Sun

A child plays in an idyllic landscape. The sun blazes above; over-arching all is the starry sky.

The Cosmos The sun has been worshiped throughout history, and no wonder, for its very light can nurture or destroy mortals. Unpitying sunlight forms deserts and wastelands. The depletion of our natural sun shield, the ozone layer of the atmosphere, has made the rays of the sun more carcinogenic. The sun is also the bringer of health, a universal disinfectant and healer. Organisms hostile to human life, such as bacteria, mold, and mildew, are often defeated by the heat and light of the sun. Mental depression can be alleviated by exposure to sunlight.

In past centuries, people in the West perceived the earth as being at the center of the cosmos. The center of awareness later shifted and now we place the sun at the center of our solar system, though the universe is not known to have a center—or a

61

boundary. The sun is the center of "our world" as we know it: a constant flux of creation, maintenance, and destruction.

The Human Community   Archetypically, the sun represents the ability to reason, to assess facts, to be objective. The rational mind is a valid, valuable part of the human psyche, but the light of reason can be a merciless ray. Intolerance for "foolish" sentiment, as well as hidebound academia, rigid philosophies that codify a flawed status quo, the ideal of the self-sufficient, complacent "self-made man" are examples of social sunburn. An over-solarized society is less inclined to sympathize with those who are down and out, and more inclined to rationalize stinginess and alienation. What doesn't fit into the culture's rosy self-image will be mocked or suppressed. Lunar types arouse mass psychosis; the heat of solar passion, often disguised as rational "solutions" to social problems, energizes mobs to act on the lunacy.

Tempered by compassion and insight, the rational mind is a priceless treasure. The Constitution of the United States was framed by men whose value of reason and knowledge transcended self-interest and personal emotional considerations. The insightful, rational mind allows us to see that prejudice is based on fear and negative conditioning. As the intuitive mind turns toward the unknown, reason prompts us to investigate.

Science has gifted us with advances in disease control. For example, simple concepts of hygiene now taken for granted were inspired by the revelations of the microscope. Educational and scientific institutions and doctors who rely on empiricism and technology are in the realm of the sun.

The child on the card indicates that innocence and candor are also fostered by the sun. These qualities translate into openness and accountability in governments and institutions, and patriotism inspired by equitable government. Whereas the Strength card refers to the might of the armed forces and police, the Sun card focuses on the honor, bravery, and glamour these institutions can have.

The Individual   The sun can shine with brilliant intensity; the solar type can be filled with passion. Unlike the Piscean/lunar type, a sun child will not hide or be lost in his or her emotions. The solar type relishes sharing all with everyone, and natural charisma ensures an eager and devoted audience. Leo, ruled by the sun, is the astrological sign most connected with show business.

Like lunar qualities, solar qualities are beautiful when balanced. Objectivity is warmed by patriotism and loyalty. Reason is deepened with intuition; a sense of right and wrong is graced by compassion. Tibetan Buddhist iconography represents the moon as the soothing, cooling effect of compassion on the troubled mind, whereas the sun represents the fearless and intense quality of wisdom that burns away the obscurations that prevent us from realizing the wondrous nature of the mind.

The Sun card indicates a balanced, objective person with a strict sense of honor. As a companion, this person will be passionate but discreet, and honest—sometimes painfully so. The Sun can herald a flamboyant person, a teller of tall tales, an entertaining and charming braggart. The glare of the spotlight is to this person rays of beneficent sunshine. Fearlessness is a trait that all solar types share; the Sun may bring a dare-devil, a soldier, or anyone who is unafraid to fight for their cause, or for a share of the loot. The Sun can be a physician, as was Asclepius, son of the Greek solar god Apollo. The Sun generally points to good health. Children are born under the benevolence of the sun. The Sun card may indicate children born to a woman who is past her child-bearing prime.

Meanings: Light. Openness. Completion. Warmth. Satisfaction. Energy. Idealism. Passion. Education. Science. Patriotism. Bravery. Honor. Children. Medicine. A physician. Contentment. Joy. A happy marriage. A good friend. High spirits. Sincerity. Achievement in the arts. Arrogance. Loneliness. Cloudy outlook.

JUDGEMENT

XX Judgement

Three trumpets reach from the cosmos to wake the dead. Two women and a man spring from the parched soil. A manacle breaks away from one of the women's wrists. A spectrum of light is cast from the sun.

The Cosmos Judgement depicts the end—the end of a cosmic cycle, or the end of the cosmos altogether—and the beginning of something new. The miracle takes place all the time. A seed falls to the ground and decays, and a plant pushes its way to the light. The flood that destroys all in its path leaves a rich, nurturing silt when it recedes.

Judgement represents not only the end of place, of material existence, but also the end of time. How can we conceive this? How to understand? All but the most realized beings have no more idea of timelessness, or eternity, than an acorn has of an oak—though the unfolding of enlightenment is encoded within each of us, as the oak is in the acorn.

The Human Community A Buddhist teaching says, "If you want to know what you were in a past life, look in the mirror." What has come into being sprang from the past, just as the immortals on the card are reborn in human form. For example, even strong democracies tend to focus on single leaders—presidents or prime ministers—as our ancestors bowed to kings and queens.

We build from ancient materials, often without realizing it. The great Indian statesman, Jawaharlal Nehru said, "We are all, individuals as well as nations, products of our past (call it heredity or the cumulative effect of action) and our environments. To that extent, and it is a great deal, we are children of destiny, bound in many ways to walk along a predetermined path." The thought blends the feeling of X Wheel of Fortune, the half-way point to XX Judgement, and the Judgement card.

As we evaluate the past by examining the present, so the future will be defined by the present. Nehru spoke of destiny not as ordained by gods, but rather as inherited from formations of the past. Equality or inequity, freedom or oppression, prosperity or disparity of wealth—we leave these to our children, our grandchildren, their children. The generations to come will be our ultimate judge.

The Individual The resurrection of the body is a tenet of most sects of Christianity, and the image of people in physical forms rising from tombs and graves is familiar in Western art. People of many other religions and cultures have focused attention on after-death survival of the physical body, as evidenced by the development of the science of embalming and customs of making material offerings to the dead.

One could say that all this attention to the after-death body is simply a fear of extinction. We are very much in love with our bodies, unless extreme pain or some form of renunciation changes us. But the idea of a resurrected body is compelling beyond a mere wish for survival.

We are not souls with bodies as dangling appendages, nor are our processes all physical. Whether we believe in reincarnation and karma, or in one lifetime that is judged by a god, or in a life with no after-death existence, it is obvious that body and mind are interdependent. What we do with our bodies imprints on our souls (streams of consciousness) and vice versa. This is karma, or judgement. The traces left in our minds by good or evil actions condition us to gravitate toward good or evil, love or hate, compassion or self-centeredness.

Judgement forces us to confront the consequences of our actions, physical and mental. Patterns created throughout life now solidify and are held up for evaluation. The final reckoning has come, whether one is ready for it or not.

In a day to day sense, Judgement indicates a transformation or breakthrough. A sense of suffocating frustration gives way to fresh air and problems solved. Abilities that have been hidden come to light. One is permeated with a delightful feeling of renewal, of rebirth and rejuvenation.

Meanings: Breakthrough. Transformation. Waking up latent powers. Atonement. Judgement. The need to repent and forgive. Rejuvenation. Rebirth. Promotion. The need to consider how one's actions affect others. Stagnation. Legal settlement. Sense of breaking free of old repressions.

THE WORLD

XXI The World

A woman dances on a globe in the midst of the cosmos, surrounded by an angel, an eagle, a bull, and a lion. Roses stream around her, off into the stars. She holds a shepherd's crook in her hands.

The World, of all the cards of the tarot, most integrates all that has gone before and all that is to come. Like the other Major Arcana, the World card is interpreted by sections—"The Cosmos," "The Human Community," and "The Individual"—all of which outline facets of our lives. The metaphysical shines into human life; the society in which we live affects the most private areas of our lives. Each card of the Major Arcana should be seen as an integrated whole, but the World card especially exemplifies this.

The Cosmos The World is the circle within the circle, and the circle around the circle. It is the womb of the Fool, the cosmos fully realized.

The dancing movement of the human body, costumed and masked, or naked, reflects the movement of creation and destruction. The deity Shiva is portrayed as Lord of the Dance, dancing in cosmic fire. A Quaker hymn calls Jesus, too, Lord of the Dance. Medieval Europe embraced a genre of art in which victims of the plague are shown following the grim reaper in a *danse macabre.* The rhythm of dance is the rhythm of life and death, of the seasons, of the breath of animals, people, and deities.

The Cosmic Tarot

The creatures that surround the dancer are symbolic of the four elements: angel is air, eagle is water, bull is earth, and lion is fire. (The European genesis of the tarot is seen also in the fact that the animals are symbolic of the four Gospel writers: Matthew, angel; John, eagle; Luke, bull; and Mark, lion. The shepherd's crook in the woman's hands also hints at an identification with Christ.)

The World shows the unity of end and beginning. The joy of the dance calls us to earthly existence, while the cosmos invites us to explore the unknown that lies beyond.

The Human Community Sacred dance has been all but lost to the sanctuaries of mainstream Western religions, but elsewhere it has a strong place: dance as possession by deity or demon; dance in praise, fellowship, or propitiation; dance as meditation; dance as reenactment of the drama of deities and demons; dance as healing rite.

Dance in any context can be an act of joy: in a discotheque, at a prayer meeting, at a wedding, in a ballroom, in solitude. When (former) Yugoslavia was occupied by the Turks, the people were forbidden to play musical instruments. They fastened coins and bells to their clothes, and in dance made music.

The world is filled with suffering, and the miracle of joy happens again and again. Dancing, weeping, laughing, and hugging are spontaneous discoveries of the tender love we have for each other.

The Individual The Cosmic Tarot, in showing a beautiful and voluptuous woman dancing in the cosmos, brings the body to a divine level while losing nothing of the sensuous appeal of the dance. Experience is blended with innocence, the two not conflicting but complementary.

The World card indicates completion: of a work of art, of school, of a business deal, of a term of pregnancy. All has been gathered and united. The result may awe even the creator. Celebrate!

Meanings: Synthesis of the elements. The cosmic dance.
Unity. Understanding. Perfect application of what has been
learned. Completion. A wedding. Perfection. Success. Fulfillment.
The rewards of hard work. Forgetting the center. Fear of
devotion. Inertia. Restricted views. Lack of commitment.
Lack of vision.

• The Minor Arcana •

THE MINOR ARCANA CARDS SHIFT THE DECK from the larger themes of the Major Arcana to focus on ourselves as we exist day to day. People we have known, childhood, jobs, romances, family, friends, enemies, housing, emotional states, projects artistic and monetary, and financial situations are in the four suits of the Minor Arcana. The Minor Arcana deal with our personal lives, our ambitions, hopes, and fears, and especially direct attention to our relations with other people.

This focus does not imply that our personal lives are too minor to be concerned with the cosmos or civilization. The Major Arcana have implications for the individual, and the Minor Arcana have implications for the world at large. Both sets of Arcana work together, and in a reading all cards, Major and Minor, form a whole, a continuum.

The texts for the numbered Minor Arcana aim at creating a mood or ambience; the court cards center on people. Meanings are given as a guide for different interpretations. By casting oneself into the atmosphere of the cards during a reading or study, one discovers the meanings as they apply to the situation now, and to oneself or another person for whom one might be reading.

As in the Major Arcana, the pronoun he or she corresponds to the person or people pictured on the cards. The interpretations are inclusive of man and woman.

The suits of the Minor Arcana of the Cosmic Tarot match the four elements: wands correspond to fire, cups to water, swords to air, and pentacles to earth. The symbolism of the elements makes the Minor Arcana as a whole more comprehensible and helps the cardreader to absorb the meanings of the cards.

Suit of Wands: Fire

The fire element is the realm of the spirit. As fire consumes wood and rises higher and higher, so spiritual activity expands at the expense of materialism. Fire is the ultimate purifier; needless to say, it is also the ultimate destroyer. Passionate devotion can purge selfishness; fanaticism damns all dissent.

Religion is not necessarily the only outlet for what is labeled here as spirituality. The quest for truth unstained by arrogance or self-righteousness, and the urge to be truly compassionate, are in the realm of the spiritual, whether one is a believer, an atheist or an agnostic.

Fire gives off the creative spark, the light of inspiration. It is the birthplace of the muses. Pride is a trait of the suit of wands, as is anger.

Suit of Cups: Water

Water is the realm of the emotions, that fluid and very uncertain element of our psyches. Nothing is more mutable than water, except possibly our emotions. When emotions are in full flow, it seems that nothing can stand up to them. Judgement, prudence, and "well-laid plans" are swept away by floods of feeling.

Love is the strongest and most motivating of affections. Nothing but love can lead us to cast away self-interest, and yet love—or what is perceived as love—can lead to violent obsessions and the most devious manipulations. Love fulfilled gives us wings; unrequited love fills days and nights with tears. The Franz Liszt composition "Liebestraum," Dream of Love, musically captures the beauty of love, together with its tensions and uncertainties. Many of the cards of the suit of cups show people enjoying love, dreaming of love, or suffering from love.

Confidence, the more reliable sister of pride, is a character trait of the suit of cups, as is susceptibility and malleability.

Suit of Swords: Air

Air is the realm of the intellect. As in the expressions "mental acuity" and "sharp wits," swords symbolize the power of the mind in its rational mode.

Pain, mental and physical, is a disturbing motif in the suit of swords. "The mind is its own place, and in itself/Can make a Heav'n of Hell, a Hell of Heav'n." The words have a noble tinge, but they are spoken by Satan cast out of heaven, in John Milton's great work *Paradise Lost*. Perhaps Milton is trying to show the intellect's tendency to pretend that the causes of suffering are somehow ultimately good (for example, violence is stimulating and shows the "survival of the fittest"), and to reject or fantasize away the actions we must take to make our lives truly happy.

Mental activity does not bring only pain and delusion. The swords cards also depict situations in which explosive emotionality is tempered by reason. The intellect is the key actor in integrating emotions, body, and spirit.

Aridness and infertility are possible problems in the suit of swords. They are balanced by the ability to make full use of one's faculties and the ability to impregnate.

Suit of Pentacles: Earth

Earth is the realm of the physical and material. Whereas wands are concerned with our spiritual nature, cups with emotions, and swords with mental life, pentacles place us squarely in our bodies. The suit of pentacles, traditionally called coins, deals with all that concerns the maintenance and satisfaction of the body: food, jobs, shelter, sex, and so on. Failure and success, poverty and riches—earth offers us both sides of the coin. The settings of the other suits tend to be exotic and even surreal, but most of the pentacles cards show down-to-earth places.

The symbolic qualities of earth, along with those of water, are most fascinating to religion and psychology. (Interestingly, in the West, these elements are considered "feminine.") Perhaps it is the lure as well as the mystery of earth and water that draw the focus of churchmen and analysts. Religions advise us to restrict earthy sensuality and watery emotions. Many schools of psychology tell us that we must indulge our emotional and physical urges, as if these are dangerous substances that must be siphoned off to maintain certain hygienic levels.

As in the other elemental realms, it is balance or imbalance of physical concerns that provides the outcome. A person obsessed with gathering riches places himself or herself in danger of being without inner resources in emotional or material crises. Continuing in a detested job for the sake of personal wealth is to make oneself no different from an ox pulling a plough, dreaming of the trough of hay at sundown. On the other hand, if a hated job is endured out of love, perhaps to support children or parents or friends, then one yokes oneself to the unselfish heart, and this is the greatest task we can give ourselves.

Stubbornness, retentiveness, and dullness are dangers in the suit of pentacles; they are offset by determination and a true concern for others' physical welfare.

The schemes of the suits, of the elements, are only that: schemes. The psyche and body cannot be cut into neat pieces. All the parts overlap and intermingle; they are interdependent, sometimes indistinguishable. The human experience is difficult to see as a whole, and the elements/suits offer a method of examining ourselves, of seeing into our motivations, needs, relationships, and so on. We should not be like the child who, having taken apart a machine, does not know how to put it back together and is confronted with a pile of useless plastic and metal bits. A whole, healthy man or woman at home with others and in the world is the ideal.

The Numbers of the Tarot

Ace symbolizes integrity, the ego, accomplishment, and beginnings. The number one is the loneliness that impels creation. It is the head of any venture or scheme.

Two is partners: the lovers, mother and father, yin and yang. Two can herald conflict or resolution, meetings and decisions. Two has a tinge of sterility: the deal has been made, inspiration has struck, but nothing is yet produced.

Three signifies the fruits of partnership: father, mother, and child; artist, media, and creation; invention, means of production, and product. Joy is felt, but it may be fleeting or mutable.

Four is foundation: family established in a home. Completion and stability are indicated, but also stasis and even stagnancy. Four evokes a feeling that one is unassailable; four can be a fort.

Five denotes conflict. External, uncontrollable elements have intruded on the four-square house. The status quo established with four is under attack.

Six brings us to a new plane. Six is three doubled; the family has been established, subjected to stress, and has discovered its own strength. Some wariness remains; security is tempered with awareness of the vicissitudes of life.

Seven represents more flux, change, and inevitably tension. The balance established in six is disrupted. Struggle or exploration can begin, or one can let go and begin to deteriorate. Whether a change is for the better or worse, it takes its toll on peace of mind.

Eight, like six, is another relatively stable place, but unlike four, eight does not foster complacency. Defensive rigidity or exhilaration at having learned from experiences can develop with eight.

Nine means we're almost there—wherever "there" is. Nine can produce feelings of tension, of powers exerted, of expectation; or there can be premature despair at bad prospects, or the fear that there are just too many loose ends to tie up.

Ten is completion, the end of a road. All influences have been exerted and we have only to look around to see the outcome. Ten does not mean that we should feel stuck if we don't like the situation in which we find ourselves. However, ten may be telling us to take a different approach. If the outcome is good, enjoy and move on.

The Court Cards

Three major factors are in play with the court cards: suit, rank, and elemental or astrological attribute.

The suit, as in all Minor Arcana cards, gives the overall outlook on the card in terms of the elements and what realm of the human psyche we are in.

The ranks of the cards tend to denote the age range of the individual indicated, as well as another elemental attribute. Princesses (called pages in traditional tarot decks) and princes (knights) can be seen as women and men with youthful qualities. Kings and queens represent men and women who are more mature, more settled and in control of their lives. Princesses tend to have earth qualities, princes fire, queens water, and kings air. One should not be bound by the gender of the figure on the card when interpreting the court cards. A prince can represent a young woman; a queen can represent a mature man.

The signs of the zodiac, like the suits of the tarot, have elemental attributes. The four elements are distributed among the twelve signs of the zodiac, so that each element is assigned to three signs.

Each sign also belongs to a quadruplicity: four signs are cardinal, four are fixed, and four are mutable. The elements are distributed in each quadruplicity: of the cardinal quadruplicity, for example, one sign is a fire sign, one is air, one is water and one is earth. "The quadruplicities represent the three basic qualities of all life: creation (cardinal)—preservation (fixed)—destruction (mutable)," says Alan Oken (1980). One can arrive at different personality types for the quadruplicities. Cardinal signs denote creative, enterprising individuals. Fixed personalities, as the word implies, tend to be concerned with conservation, consistency, and loyalty. Mutable signs have the characteristics of adaptability and resourcefulness.

The princesses of the Cosmic Tarot represent the element of the suit as manifest in the human personality, as well as having a basic earth quality, whatever the suit or astrological sign might be. Princes represent the fixed signs of the zodiac and have a fire quality. Queens are the mutable signs and have a water quality, and kings are the cardinal signs and have an air quality.

The court cards rarely describe a real person completely. To find ourselves or others in the courts, the attributes of the different cards must be blended in different degrees. The sign of the zodiac by which people generally identify themselves names only the influence of the sun in the astrological chart. In the same way, a court card indicates the major area of influence a person may have on the issue at hand, or the way in which a certain personality is expressed in the situation.

Rank	Princess	Prince	Queen	King
Element of Rank	Earth	Fire	Water	Air
Wands	Fire	Leo	Sagittarius	Aries
Cups	Water	Scorpio	Pisces	Cancer
Swords	Air	Aquarius	Gemini	Libra
Pentacles	Earth	Taurus	Virgo	Capricorn
Quadruplicity	—	Fixed	Mutable	Cardinal

SUIT OF WANDS

Ace of Wands

Ace of Wands

The wand of the ace blazes like a torch with energy from the starry sky. The shape of its light is contained, indicating energy channeled with purpose. Power is drawn from the cosmos down to the individual. The ace of wands signifies the element of fire.

A work of art, a prosperous business, a life-saving medicine, or a delicious dinner all require motivation and hard-headed planning. Materials must be gathered, research done, techniques perfected. But pity the person who must know the exact outcome of every action taken. Without the risk of stumbling in the dark, the "spark" of creativity will never be struck.

As the wand on the ace radiates light from an unknown source, so inspirations come from the unknown. We have ideas and plans, ideals and dreams; the ace of wands signifies the moment in which we see the way, when the form of a dream is revealed.

Meanings: Origin. Source. Inheritance. Self-realization. Creation. Beginning. Invention. Enterprise. Birth of a child. Male fertility. An adventure. False start. Cancellation. Blind power.

Two of Wands

Two of Wands

A man in the prime of life stands confidently between two wands. Light arches between the tops of the wands, and the sky itself frames the man's head. The mountains, the flock of birds, the straight lines of the trees, and the wands themselves emphasize the sky as the backdrop.

Superb pride is in every line of this man's stance. His head is high, his clothes immaculate, his feet well-poised. He has riches and status. Yet he is not complacent; his eyes are raised to lofty distances.

The two wands, rooted in the earth, shining in the air, indicate opposites: male and female, light and dark, joy and sorrow, exaltation and degradation. The man stands between them, aware but unbiased. As the composer Johannes Brahms said, "The ideal and the genuine man is calm both in his joy and in his sorrow."

Meanings: Dominion. Superiority. Authority. Success by understanding opposites. Maturity. An even temperament. Contradictory events. Sadness.

THREE OF WANDS

Three of Wands

A young woman dances, and the earth near her bursts into flower. Miraculously, three lotuses spring from the dusty ground. Above is a star; around the woman are three wands. Her beautiful, seductive clothes reveal and conceal her body as she dances, and bands of gold are on her arms and head.

The woman dances alone in an empty landscape. Her expression flows unhindered by the lack of audience. She dances for her own joy, in response to the earth below and the sky above. She is drawn to the star, even as she draws it toward herself and the earth. The three wands symbolize the act of creation, a solitary inspiration taking tangible form. The woman is an artist inspired by her vision, untouched by concerns of money or fame.

Meanings: Virtue. Growth. Success through self-confidence. Art. Dreams come true. Manifested will. Creativity. Activity. Joy of discovery. Preventing confrontations.

FOUR OF WANDS

Four of Wands

A dancer echoes the flight of a bird. Around her are four wands; in the distance are pyramids. Four white flowers grow among the wands. The earth itself spirals in harmony with the dance. Whereas the dancer on the three of wands held herself close to the earth, this dancer seems about to take off in flight.

Dancers and spectators of dance often use the metaphor of flight to describe particularly beautiful moves or even to title dance pieces. The dance piece "The Lark Ascending" by the Alvin Ailey American Dance Theatre (on the video "Ailey Dances") shows human flight without wings or machines.

The four wands and the four flowers, symbolic of earthly foundation, would seem to ground our dancer. However, it is with her earthly body that she offers us wings.

Meanings: Completion. Rise. Clarification. Peace. Joy in life. Fiery love. Exhilaration in physical activity. Guilelessness. New prosperity. Insecurity. Need to ground oneself.

FIVE OF WANDS

Five of Wands

Two men fight, using wands as weapons. Around them is a circle of rocks, and behind them is a ragged fence.

Few activities can match fighting, in terms of energy raised and expended. From religious epics to tribal wars to gang riots to adventure movies to boxing matches: we are fascinated with violence. Battles, mock or real, are considered by many to be an initiation into manhood.

The circle of stones around the two men gives a ritualistic air to the fight. The stones and the fence may contain the violence, or the violence may spill out, spreading the destruction, causing more pain and strife.

Meanings: Strife. Violence. War. Confrontation. Argument. Support. Concentrated energy push. Struggle. Labor. Escalating conflicts. Complexity. Blockade. Dilution of efforts. Images of violence and influences dangerous especially to children.

81

Six of Wands

Six of Wands

A young man kneels on the ground, holding a wand. He wears the laurel wreath of victory. A lion reclines nearby, also crowned.

The battle has been fought and now the triumph can be savored. The heat of aggression still permeates the landscape, but flowers bloom from the dry ground.

The lion is the totem of the victorious warrior, from Hercules who fought barehanded the Nemean lion, to Richard the Lionheart of Aquitaine and England. Kings of many nations have claimed the animal for their coats of arms.

The reclining lion of the six of wands has banked its ferocity for the moment. It must be guarded carefully by its youthful master, however. The strength of the beast can be useful, but power has a way of devouring those who try to exploit it without having the strength of character to control it. The sigil of Jupiter, on the youth's tunic, indicates that wisdom tames aggression.

Meanings: Victory. Forces in balance. Success. Hope. Conquest. A solid team with a strong leader. Triumph. Good news. Advance. Desires realized as a result of efforts. Anxiety. Inconclusive gain. Treachery from a subordinate. Mutiny.

SEVEN OF WANDS

Seven of Wands

A man in front of a fence heroically defends himself against six rods. His survival will depend on skill and courage.

Everyone at some point must deal with a bully. Confronted with overwhelming strength, we fall back on inner resources: wit, brazenness, courage, sheer panache. Sometimes diplomacy works; sometimes we resort to elaborate but empty threats.

The martial arts favor not brute strength, but mental and physical flexibility. Concentration, bravery, tranquility, focus, and mental acuity, as well as physical dexterity and strength are heroic traits. The seven of wands indicates the ability to harness all of one's skills to overcome adversity.

Meanings: Overwhelming odds surmounted. Valor. Action without planning. Negotiation. Contest. Fight for survival. Skill in martial arts. Courage. Worry. Agitation. Hesitation may cause losses. Perplexity.

EIGHT OF WANDS

Eight of Wands

A man flies through the air, his legs extended to their utmost. He exults in the swiftness of his flight. The four wands above him act as lightning rods, drawing down the powers of the sky. The man does not appear to be fleeing from something or rushing toward something. He represents energy for the sake of energy, the burst of enthusiasm that comes even before a purpose or an action is clearly formulated.

Eventually, the man will have to slow down and pace himself if he is not to exhaust himself before he completes his travels. The exhilaration he is now experiencing, however, will carry him far.

Meanings: Swift activity. Sudden progress or movement. Enthusiasm. New solutions. Speed. Hastily made decisions. Too rapid advancement. Thorns of dispute. Jealousy. Doubt. Remorse. Burn out.

NINE OF WANDS

Nine of Wands

A muscular and masculine youth gazes steadfastly into the distance. His hair stands up, as if it is too energized to lie flat. A lion behind him is screened by five transparent wands. Four wands are in front of the youth. One is twined by a thin serpent.

The serpent and the lion are both symbols of power. Snakes can represent the energy of the body as acted on by the mind. Lions indicate physical strength and prowess. As the youth stands between the lion and the serpent, it is up to him to gain access to their potency. He must not be blinded by fantasies of his own strength.

Meanings: Anticipation. Self-determination. Discipline. Order. Revealed passions. Knowledge, or lack of knowledge, of one's own strength. A pause in a current struggle. Obstacles. Adversity. Delay. Tension.

TEN OF WANDS

Ten of Wands

The ten of wands presents an image of disaster: a world burning, a person caught in the flames. Wrecked buildings give an unmistakable picture of war. Saturn, considered by many to be a baleful influence, is visible through the clouds of smoke.

All of us are responsible for our country's government—and for all human governments. Silent acquiescence can be the signature on a contract with tyranny. As Dr. Martin Luther King said, "To ignore evil is to become an accomplice to it."

The figure trapped by the wands might be a victim of his or her own passiveness, or this person might be one who sacrificed his or her life to the cause of liberty, which is never lost, even if it is at times obscured.

Meanings: Oppression. Last effort. Excessive pressures. Link between strongly opposing elements. Stubbornness. Burden. Difficulties. War. Losses. Displacement. Fulfillment of great wishes. New expectations from life.

PRINCESS OF WANDS

Princess of Wands

A young woman gazes at us from a tropical landscape. Behind her, as if in reflection of her sultry eyes, the sun burns over a volcano. The princess symbolizes the element of fire. The ornament on her headdress resembles the trident of the Hindu deity Shiva (see XI Strength).

The princess of wands is well aware of her power to attract, though she may not be mature enough to maintain a relationship. She represents an energetic person who takes chances, who might jump into a situation without examining it. This person angers quickly and forgives quickly. She may say or do things that are later regretted, but she will go to extravagant measures to make up. In a relationship, the princess of wands is passionately attached to the good opinion of her partner. Though she seems to dominate, behind the scenes she may be at the mercy of the other.

Inspiration drives the princess. She will drop everything (and everyone) in order to pursue her artistic vision. She tends, also, to dump her friends when a new romance sparks her. Her passions are intense and run a quick course, often with high damages.

Understanding and patience go a long way in a friendship with the princess. She does not mean to test those who love her, and hurting others saddens her more than injuries to herself. The influence of a strong, quiet type can moderate her fiery impulsiveness, as she is amenable to good counsel.

Meanings: Spontaneity. Energy. A person willing to accept risks. Impulsiveness. Passion in both love and anger. An artist. An envoy. A stranger with good intentions. A bearer of important news. Superficiality. Instability. A heartbreaker.

PRINCE OF WANDS

Prince of Wands

A youth bears a club and a shield. Though his shield reflects a lion, the youth shows no fear. Like the princess of wands, the prince wears a headdress on which is the trident of Shiva. Under the collar of his jacket is the sigil of the astrological sign Leo. The sun and the lion are symbols of Leo.

If Aries is the head of the zodiac, Leo is the heart. To have the heart of a lion is to be bold, generous, loyal to friends, and implacable to enemies. The prince of wands advances fearlessly into situations, trusting his own resources and trusting his supporters. Whatever the prince does will be done with flair and panache, as Leo likes "putting on the Ritz." A love of showmanship can degenerate into conceit, and the prince becomes a poseur. Gold is his metal: he may be a gold-tone phony, or he may be genuine and untarnished, bright and warm. When secure in his self-esteem, the prince shares all with all.

Like other felines, the Leonine prince has a well-developed sense of pride. When compromised, he will snarl and maybe even snap.

The term "pride" also applies to the lion's offspring. The prince is an affectionate and generous parent, and his children are likely to be as shining as he is. The prince may indicate the birth of a grandchild, or an important occasion concerning a grandchild.

Meanings: Strength. Nobility. Trust. Righteousness. Bravery. Style. Humor. Friendliness. Warmth. Intense love. Parental love. Pride. Grandchildren. Advance into the unknown. Flight. Pretentiousness. Intolerance. Prejudice.

QUEEN OF WANDS

Queen of Wands

The queen of wands is an authoritative woman. Her tiara and jeweled gown and her beauty give her an air of glamour. She holds a bouquet of white flowers, symbolizing purity of heart. In the background is a tower on which an archer guards the approaches from the sea.

The archer symbolizes Sagittarius. Jupiter, ruler of Sagittarius, is king of the gods, and the queen symbolizes a woman who, in spite of society's prejudices, can rule men and women. Her strength comes not from being "an honorary man" (to quote writer Ursula K. LeGuin), but from her character and quality. She evokes great loyalty in her subjects, who consider her valuable and irreplaceable.

The queen of wands can represent a person who seems larger than life. Physically, in fact, she probably is Rubenesque. If she is an artist, she will work on a large scale. Monuments and operas are more to her taste than miniatures and kitchen-sink dramas. She goes for all the gusto she can get, and though she is never out of control, she can embarrass more timid or reserved companions. She enjoys activities whose challenges and arenas are large, for example, exploring, sky-diving, mountain climbing, ocean swimming.

The queen's inclination is to stride over what she considers petty. She can be callous, but if she uses her powerful mental facilities with sensitivity, she can show us a world that transcends selfish, spirit-deadening trivialities.

Meanings: A sympathetic and understanding person. Glamour. Honor. Friendliness. Loving and kind person. Executive abilities. Strong will. Enthusiasm. Sports. Travel. Vengefulness.

King of Wands

King of Wands

The king of wands bears a wand and a red tulip. In the background is a standard on which is the symbol of Aries.

Aries, the top of the zodiac, rules with the head. The king's intellect rules over his emotions and physical appetites—or he may be merely headstrong. He finds it difficult to accept loss, and his main weakness is in his denial of personal weakness. A situation that offers no resolution may find the king butting his head against the wall, or the king may be the one who leads others through a period of despair and into the light.

Because he acts in the fiery realm of quick energy, the king, like his Libran counterpart the king of swords, can be long on inspiration and ideas and short on follow-through. The proud tenacity of the king can overrule his lack of perseverance, enabling him to find the breach in the wall and lead the way through it.

If the wish to dominate takes hold of him, the king of wands will be ruthless. If he devotes his natural warmth and fiery enthusiasm and energy to the service of others, he will realize greatness. Aries is the least materialistic sign of the zodiac, and his ability to tolerate hardship can put him on the front lines of humanitarian work. Like his mate, the Sagittarian queen of wands, the king loves adventures and challenge. Since, for him, the end supports the means, and because he is generally fearless, he is the quintessential guerrilla warrior, smuggler, or pirate; he will volunteer for the "dust off" operation of rescuing wounded personnel behind enemy lines. He will stop at nothing to accomplish his mission; emergency services and investigative or combat journalism are good uses of his energy. He may also be attracted to explosives and firearms.

Everyone pays attention when the king of wands walks into a room, such is the force of his personality. Acquaintances admire more than love him, but from the people who are close to him he receives deep devotion, which he returns in full. The soft pink and lavender colors of the king's clothes indicate sensitivity.

The king may be a man who is past the prime of life but has retained his potency; he may be a man who has married late in life. The king is naturally strong; his fiery metabolism means that he is probably lean as well.

Meanings: Vivid personality. Strong will. Adventurer. Conscientiousness. Creativity. Charisma. Generosity. Tenacity. Ascetic type. Devotion. Friendliness. An educated person. A gentleman. Austerity. Carpe diem. Excessive and exaggerated ideas. Impetuousness.

SUIT OF CUPS

ACE OF CUPS

Ace of Cups

A golden chalice underwater over-flows with liquid and light. The moon and stars throw brilliant rays into the starry sky. The emotions of life touch the realm of the earth, as signified by the soil on which the cup stands. Overflowing joy and an ocean of tears are contained in the cup.

Twelve stars above the cup sym-bolize completion in the "base twelve" number system. The fellow-ship of Christ's apostles numbered twelve, Hercules performed twelve labors, the zodiac has twelve houses, day and night have twelve hours each. Gareth Knight, in *Qabalistic Symbolism,* calls the signs of the zodiac "markers on a great clock which serve to indicate the type of force emanating from the Solar Logos at any particular time." (By Solar Logos, Knight means "the Conditioner and Sustainer of our Solar System.")

Twelve is a number of time, a reminder of how impermanent the most deeply felt emotions can be. As religious ritual uses water to wash away impurity or sinfulness, mundane and fleeting emotions can be transformed into divine compassion.

Meanings: Abundance. Fulfillment. Perfection. Joy. Female fertility. Beauty and pleasure. Goodness overflowing. Favorable outlook. Change. Erosion. Instability. Inconstancy.

Two of Cups

Two of Cups

A man and a woman kiss in a cinematic fantasy scene. Flowers float all around them, and two chalices exchange light. The chalices contain cold liquid—maybe the drink of lovers, champagne. The cosmos evokes the floating feeling that a lover's embrace can bring.

Romantic love inspires more expression in the arts than anything else. It is an ancient celebration and a most delightful event.

If the lovers stay together, the end of the "honeymoon period" will change their relationship. They will learn to live with each other's faults and idiosyncrasies, and the affair will deepen into an enduring love; or they will separate to chase new butterflies.

The scene on the two of cups depicts the moment when two people discover passion between themselves. They may have been friends for a while; they may have just met. The future is unclear—and in this blissful moment, the lovers have no thought for it.

The two of cups can also signify the joyful beginning of a new friendship or the decision to commit to a relationship, whether business, romantic, or platonic.

Meanings: Love and its uniting power. Strong links. Friendship beginning or renewed. Passion. Union. Harmony. Engagement. Cooperation. Partnership. Unsatisfactory love. Conflicting emotions. False friendship. Troubled relationship. Star-crossed love.

THREE OF CUPS

Three of Cups

A man in tights and a woman in dance costume gracefully pose at the edge of a lake. Three overflowing chalices are before them. Beyond the lake is a landscape of mountains and waterfalls. The abundance of flowing water in the scene signifies purity and healing; the still water of the lake signifies contemplation and rest.

New lovers can be the most self-absorbed of people, aware of nothing but their own pleasures. When the first gush of love is tempered and the lovers again become aware of the world, their love for each other can bring cheer to others who might be lonely or sad, and can be an immense source of creative activity. In this way, the exclusiveness of the couple gives way to their dance.

The three of cups indicates the ability to share gifts of grace and talent. A special dance, theater, or music performance may be in the offing.

Meanings: The arts, especially performing arts. Abundance. Exuberance. Comfort. Bliss. Pleasure. Solace. Healing. Excessive pleasures. Overabundance. Superfluity.

FOUR OF CUPS

Four of Cups

A youth reclines beside a pond. Although his surroundings are pleasant, he seems lost in thought. A white horse grazes in the background and a castle is in the distance. Wine and fruit are on the cloth. Four lotuses with cups are unseen by the youth.

Prosperity and leisure are the gifts of the youth's life. Everything is offered to him. A needy person might pay more attention to the cups, but perhaps this young man is weary of an unchallenging life in which all his needs are met by others. The horse offers adventure through travel; the lotuses reflect the voyage inward. The youth remains unaware, lost in his ennui.

The four of cups indicates an opportunity of which one has not the energy to be aware, or privileges that are taken for granted rather than appreciated. It can warn of the danger of over-planning—spending too much time thinking while the opportunity to act passes. A spoiled and jaded young person may enter the scene. Alternatively, the four of cups can indicate the discovery of new approaches to old problems or the patience to wait until a situation is ripe. A youth may provide inspiration for resolving what have seemed to be intractable difficulties.

Meanings: Weariness. Uncertainty. Decaying joy. Refusal. Aversion. Disgust. Disappointment. Stationary period in life. New possibilities. Insight. New relationships. New approaches to old problems. Anticipation. Patience.

Five of Cups

Five of Cups

A woman bowed with depression sits at a table upon which are five over-turned cups. Memories of rejected love are symbolized in the broken, unopened flower bud. The spilled liquor is lost joy. The weather outside the open door of her home is stormy.

The woman broods, savoring her remorse and sorrow. The dark walls of her house seem to close around her, just as her body posture is tight and closed. Her life has been without risk; or perhaps she took her chances, wisely or foolishly, and lost.

Memories can be a burden or a comfort in times of oppression, or they can serve as lessons. They cannot take the place of life. The door is open, and though the weather is inhospitable, perhaps some new hope will come into the woman's life, along with the dead leaves of the past season.

The cards five of cups and four of cups mirror each other. The four of cups shows a youth whose cups are too full; the five shows a woman whose cups are empty. Both people find no joy in the reality of the present. The five of cups warns of depression and gloomy nostalgia. One may be cultivating regrets or self-recriminations that bear only bitter fruit.

The past may bring delight to the present: a meeting with an old friend, the rediscovery of a favorite place or activity, renewal of strength or of one's childhood faith.

Meanings: Remorse. Regret. Marriage of convenience. Inheritance. Hopeful outlook. Return of an old friend. Reunion. Discovery of inner resources.

Six of Cups

Six of Cups

A youth and a young woman sit among rushes, six cups around them. Their faces are vague and composed in spite of the erotic intimacy of their clothing and pose.

Water, the element of the emotions, is also the element of dreams. Fluid and changing, dreams reflect our thoughts and fantasies and the impressions made on our senses.

The lovers at the lake are dreaming. Each is the fantasy of the other, with features drawn from real-life lovers of the past, adored but unattainable present-day persons, pop or film stars, music, poetry, and whatever else feeds the romantic fancy. They do not actually touch each other, even in the "kiss." All is in the realm of what-might-be.

The six of cups signifies innocent dreams of love and romance. It is the Sleeping Beauty, the tender heart protected by a castle of fantasy. The heart that guards its sleep for too long will wither, but adolescent dreams can feed contemplation in later years, and at least make a difficult phase of life more happy. All of the accoutrements of romance, from playful Valentines to melancholy symphonies, are contained in the six cups.

Meanings: Effortless harmony. Joy. Satisfaction. Nice memories. Recovered joy. Fantasies. Infatuation. A secret admirer. The culture of romance. Renewal. Chance. Remembrance. Longing. Uncontrolled emotions.

SEVEN OF CUPS

Seven of Cups

A man crouching on the ground is tormented by phantasms and fantasies. The seven cups erupt with figments of imagination.

The central image echoes the six of cups. A nightmare comes forth from the dream. Love has been unrequited or rejected, and the memory of past hopes is agony. In the reversal of his feelings, the man is enslaved by resentment and desire, and in his mind the woman is a witch, with wand, pentacle, book, dagger, and flames. The rose of love in the foreground sheds its petals, and the worm-filled cup in the ground hints at corruption.

A crown, the dream of wealth and authority, is the only thing that remains bright. In such a way, the embittered cynic is self-convinced that riches and power are worth more than love.

The seven of cups warns of feelings that become perversions— negative conditioning through negative fantasy. Replacing reality with dreams causes enervation, exhaustion, apathy, and even psychotic delusions.

However unpleasant or confusing dreams might be, they offer clues to our psychological makeup. Sometimes, too, unbridled fantasy offers inspirations. "Brain-storming" can be the best way to start a project. The seven of cups can indicate that important work is happening in the psyche.

Meanings: Illusion. Imagination. Daydreams. Wishful thinking. Disillusionment. Ruin. Delusions. Illusory success. Hopes and fears. Dream work. Productive power of fantasy.

Eight of Cups

Eight of Cups

A dejected man sits at the edge of a lake. Behind him is a wrecked, decaying boat. The rotted pier on which he sits is scattered with cups, some overturned, some still upright.

The man may have completed his journey, or was not able even to begin. Long-held hopes have soured to disappointment.

The eight of cups indicates a blow to one's self-confidence and self-esteem, perhaps the loss of a job or of backing for a project. Someone whose support was treasured may have departed.

What one does now will determine whether the situation improves or deteriorates. Accepting circumstances and personal limitations may lead to other solutions. Depression and apathy are natural reactions to setbacks, but should they continue to deepen, it's time to get solid support and help from family and friends. A shift of focus from accomplishment to process can help: the work itself can be more rewarding than its actual fruit. The eight of cups can indicate failure to make the effort to complete a project, even when all signs are pointing to success. Lack of confidence, lack of encouragement, and laziness are obstacles.

Meanings: Resignation. Giving up. Discouragement. Disappointment. Abandonment of plans. Shyness. Lack of self-esteem. Modesty. Interruption. Lethargy. Indolence. Regrouping. Seeking new support. New point of view.

NINE OF CUPS

Nine of Cups

The nine of cups is commonly called the Wish Card. The image on the Cosmic Tarot shows a handsome man approaching a lovely woman who wears a headdress with roses. The couple is surrounded by glowing cups. In the distance is water, the medium of love, and further away are mountains. The sun's intensity is veiled by clouds, creating a peaceful glow.

The upturned face of the woman is like the golden chalices around her: a receptacle of light and quiet joy. In her rapture she seems almost unaware of the man who leans to kiss her brow. The man is in shadow, unobtrusive and sensitive to her meditation.

The image brings to mind the tale of Sleeping Beauty: the virginal woman waiting in sleep for the kiss of the virtuous and valorous prince. The moment the kiss is given, the quiet, dreamy joy will instantly give way to something else. It is as though the cups are full to the brim, and any event will spill their contents over the edge. Much of the beauty of the image on the nine of cups is in this very imminence, the brimming joy that could give way to ecstasy.

Meanings: Happiness. Wealth. Success. Material attainment. Advantage. Well-being. Abundance. Good health. Difficulties surmounted. Sensitivity to the moods of others. The moment when satiation is imminent. Indifference. Imperfection. Insensitivity.

Ten of Cups

TEN OF CUPS

A woman rests on the edge of water in a mountainous landscape. The light is dim, diffuse. The cups overflow. The sensuous, plump woman is almost out of her element. She seems to belong in a boudoir, with curtains drawn to filter out any harshness or unflattering light.

The wilderness saves the woman from being lost in the languor of the mood. Her headcover gives her a token protection against the elements, but her body is in contact with the earth. She gazes at the overflowing cups in complete passivity. Unlike the nine of cups, the ten of cups is without anticipation of change or development. The woman is satiated; there is nothing more for her to do.

Ten is a number of completion, and ten cups means emotional fulfillment or resolution. To those with a restless temperament, this card might mean boredom and stagnation, a kind of bovine placidness and complacency. Usually, though, the ten of cups indicates a time of mellowness, when problems are vanquished or at least in abeyance. One allows oneself to let go of ambition and to sit back and enjoy family, friends, artistic activity, hobbies, and physical pleasure.

The ten of cups can also mean someone whose company is relaxing. This person excels at caring for other living beings—humans, animals, and plants—especially invalids. The touch of his or her hands is soothing.

Meanings: Perfect success. Satiety. Calm. Satisfaction.

Home. Joy. Vacation. Relaxation. Massage therapist. Nurse. Pleasure. Peace. Love. Contentment. Good family. Honor. Esteem. Virtue. Over-satiation. Boredom. Aimlessness. Disturbance after the climax. Family quarrel.

PRINCESS OF CUPS

Princess of Cups

A young woman shields a cup with her hands. A lily is in the foreground; a ship is behind. The princess is in the realm of water.

The cup under the woman's hands glows. It indicates an emotional life that is vibrant and yet sheltered, secret. The archetype of a young girl's dreams—tender, sexless fantasies—is more fiction than reality. But there is innocence in the youthful psyche, whatever the gender or physical age of its possessor may be. The lily reflects the purity of a soul that has not been buffeted by the suffering of unfulfilled desires and the disillusionment of desires fulfilled.

The princess of cups indicates hopes and dreams, happy moments evoked by old movies, memories, poetry, or a long-cherished friend: the ship of dreams, the sentimental journey. In too high doses, sentimentality gives rise to miserable nostalgia or longing, or to cheap, sickeningly sweet outpourings.

The princess can indicate a pensive type, male or female, young or old, who uses study and meditation to turn away from the crudeness of mundane life. She may be a poet or a musician who favors lyricism. She can also be a youth, male or female, who is ignorant of the causes of personal suffering and yet is piercingly sensitive: a child who cries because its mother cries, a young friend who is unhappy simply in sympathy. This person can be fiercely loyal, joyous in a friend's joy, an enemy to a friend's enemies. The princess of cups symbolizes also a beloved companion in dog form.

Meanings: A studious person. Sentimental. Pensive. Thoughtful. Quiet. Tender. Romantic. Poetry. Music. Kind. Gentle. Dreamy. Sensitive. Reflective. Meditative. Loyal. A helpful person. A trustworthy worker. Distraction. Lack of focus. A flatterer.

PRINCE OF CUPS

Prince of Cups

The prince of cups is an intense young man. Obviously of nobility, by the pocket crest, he may be in princely control or he may be in a state of aristocratic dissolution. His gaze is piercing, almost hypnotic. The person represented by the prince of cups may have a sinister appearance, even if his or her intentions are blameless.

The scorpion on the prince of cups' arm symbolizes the astrological sign of Scorpio. The element of water rules Scorpio, in paradox to the scorpion's desert habitat and burning sting. Though the prince is not vindictive without a grievance, a real injury or threat will bring on the sting, which can be devastating.

Scorpio is a sign whose power is beneath the surface, like the scorpion whose sting strikes suddenly and when least expected. He will look for hidden motivations in others, as well as having a secret agenda of his own. The misty water in the background of the prince is a reflection of obscure emotions and mental schemes.

Because Scorpio rules the genitals, it is considered prone to decadence. Sexuality in itself is not vicious, however. Sex can take us to the heights of human love and to the depths of human exploitation. It is the basic currency, the basic exchange between all humans, male and female, of all races and classes, whatever the relationship may be: lovers, siblings, parent and child, friends or enemies. The power of the sexual drive can be sublimated in the quest to unite with divinity or to attain enlightenment— hence, the celibacy of some religious orders. The snake coiled on the wand, behind the prince, is a powerful phallic image, and also an image of the kundalini power rising.

The boat in the background is propelled by Anubis, the Egyptian deity who brings the souls of the dead to the hall of judgement. Men's culture often associates sexual activity with death because, in the male physique, orgasm brings the "death" of the penis and often the urge to sleep.

The prince of cups can be a young man or woman with strong sexual and emotional charisma. If a good match is made, both partners will be intensely happy; if the prince is not pleased, he will probably engineer a way to foist his partner on someone else. The prince of cups may be obsessed with physical pleasure and with having the upper hand in relationships, especially sexual relationships. He has a tendency to mix up work and pleasure, sex and power; if he's not sensitive and honorable about the object of his attentions, he could end up with a sexual harassment complaint against him.

An abundance of imagination combined with the tendency to plot can give rise to bizarre and sometimes amusing schemes— but don't laugh at the prince. A slight to his pride will not be let go lightly, and like his Taurean counterpart the prince of pentacles, the prince of cups certainly knows how to hold a grudge. By the same token, the prince's loyalty is fixed and intense: he will go to any length for a friend, even unto death.

Enemies will despise the prince's arrogance and sarcasm; acquaintances will find him cold and reserved; friends will find his love almost frighteningly intense. He is not demanding, except in one respect: those who are close to him must be able to accept and respect his passionate love.

Meanings: Mysterious person. Imagination. An invitation or opportunity. Arrival. Approach. Attraction. Inducement. Seduction. Proposal. Passion. An intense person. Haughtiness. Subtlety. Artifice. Trickery. A sly and cunning person. A swindler. A cad or "masher."

QUEEN OF CUPS

Queen of Cups

A beautiful woman at the shore of a lake holds a fan decorated with two fish and water plants. Her crown shows the symbol of yin-yang and the trident of Shiva. The Shield (Star) of David is on her necklace.

Like the queen of wands, the queen of cups has an air of glamour. She has complete confidence in her beauty and charm. The gown in which she is wrapped flows around her like water; she is comfortable and at home in the realm of the emotions.

The Star of David corresponds to the sixth sphere of the Tree of Life (see X Wheel of Fortune), which corresponds to the solar plexus and is called Beauty. As the solar plexus is the throne of the heart, it is worked on by the strongest emotions. Extreme joy, fear, anger, or sorrow create physical sensations in that nerve center. The queen of cups can bring intense emotions, from anguish to ecstasy, which can eventually settle as a source of strength and inspiration: the kiss promised on the nine of cups has been fully tasted in the ten of cups, bringing to the queen of cups mature love—full acceptance of the cycles of longing, fulfillment, and satiety.

The powerful symbols of unity worn by the queen—the trident of Shiva, the yin-yang, the star—show her as a reconciler, a diplomat, a mediator of opposites. The queen of cups can also be a "designing woman"—or man, whose surface is all charm and hospitality and whose underlying motives are to gain social position or money or to accomplish a grand seduction.

The fish on her fan symbolize the astrological sign Pisces. Like Scorpio, Pisces has his or her own agenda, working behind the scenes rather than publicly. Unlike Scorpio, who can be a poor loser when his or her plots are overturned, Pisces moves on to the next scheme with a light heart and no hard feelings.

The queen of cups is a pleasing, sweet-natured companion. While she may not be the one to initiate adventures, she will happily go along with an imaginative friend. If she is a child, her guardians should keep a sharp eye on her companions. She is the kind of person who takes a sincere delight in others' games and creations. Her impressionable nature gives her a deep appreciation of the arts; add to this the expressiveness of the water element and she may be a great artist herself, especially as a poet or an actor.

Meanings: Kindness. Grace. Beauty. Nobility. Tolerance. Mediation. Poetry. Subjectiveness. A warm-hearted and fair person. Good friend and mother. A docile child. Gift of vision. Dishonesty. Unreliability. Vice.

King of Cups

King of Cups

A crowned king stands on the terrace of his palace by the sea. The crescent on his crown, the crab on the lapel of his robe, and the shield behind his right shoulder symbolize the astrological sign of Cancer.

The king's face bears traces of many emotions in its lines and in the ambiguous set of the mouth. He looks at once sad and happy, thoughtful and abstracted. The light on the walls of the palace is that of an in-between time: dawn or dusk.

Cancer is the most fluid of the water signs. Ruled by the moon, Cancer represents the matrix of emotional life and of the indefinable feelings that are usually called intuitive or subconscious.

The spear that rises above the shield indicates an authority that comes strangely from such a tender king. Emotional sensitivity, however, is not a bar to strength and control. The person who can really feel emotions is not the same person who is swept away by them.

The king's regard toward his subjects can be benevolent—even to the point of being suffocating. A "child of the moon," as Cancer is called, can be like an overprotective, overindulgent parent, or like an ideal parent, yielding at the right time, firm at the right time. If one is looking for nurturing or sympathy, Cancer will provide an ample supply.

Cancer is the noblest and kindest of people when allowed to express full dignity. The human heart is an open book to this student of the psyche, with friendship and romantic love as the most congenial subjects. Cancer expresses himself chiefly in devotion, whether in a relationship with his friends and family or with his god or guru.

When repressed or frustrated, Cancer can give way to gossip and intrigue and a sordid interest in freakish and uncanny phenomena of human nature. Intense melancholy, with storms of uncontrollable weeping, can strike the king; at these times, his friends and family must give him all their support and help. The king of cups loves cuddling, but he can live with physical separation; what he finds unbearable is being shut out of someone's affections. As the shell is essential to the crab, a secure home is the king's priority. He may choose a career in residential architecture or interior design.

Meanings: Friendship. Polite, humane person. Gifts. Longing. Emotionality. Enthusiasm. Responsibility and creativity. Religious person. Psychologist or behaviorist. A considerate person, kind and reliable. Shelter. Liberal manner. Interest in the arts and sciences. Generosity. Indolence. Dishonesty. Melancholy. Gullible or malleable person. Artistic temperament. Double dealing. Scandal.

SUIT OF SWORDS

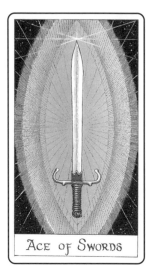

ACE OF SWORDS

Ace of Swords

A sword bathed in brilliance symbolizes the element of air. In psychological terms, air is the medium of mental activity. Swords signify conquest and power.

The triumph implied in the ace of swords is not the kind that is won by battle. All of the aces indicate "pure" elements, energy before it is given form in combination with other elements, energy on a symbolic level. The ace of swords indicates the power of the consciousness to cut through obstacles and see into its own nature.

Buddhism describes the mind as being empty, that is, as having no absolute nature in itself. It is like the sky: we believe in it, we believe that we see it, but it has no solid, graspable nature, no real attributes except what we assign to it. It is empty, like a cloud, or like a rainbow that shimmers in beauty and then disappears. What we normally call "mental" or "intellectual" are only products of conditioning and vary from being to being.

The concept of the mind truly perceiving itself is as paradoxical as an eye looking at itself. In fact, there is no mind to see or be seen. Our "self" is only a bunch of qualities assembled for a short time, a lifetime. The sword of wisdom allows us to cut through attachment to a limited ego, and find the luminosity, clarity, and emptiness of the natural "mind."

The Cosmic Tarot

In a relative or psychological sense, the sword indicates mental concerns such as reason, study, contemplation, intellect, and ideas.

Meanings: Power. Triumph. Conquest. Mental power. Great determination. An issue with many sides. Passion. Fertility. Championship. Debacle. Tyranny. Disaster. Self-destruction. Violent temper. Ambiguity. Repression.

Two of Swords

Two of Swords

A woman sits on a broken pier. A cat is beside her, the moon above. Two swords are stuck in the ground.

The water and moonlight indicate emotions; the water plants indicate waters that are rather swampy. The girl enjoys the lotus, and taps the water with one foot, careful not to stir its muddy depth. She can "visit" her emotions, but the swords of reason are nearby; she will not let herself be pulled into the swamp.

A truce has been made between emotions and intellect. An atmosphere of tranquility bathes the image, and yet this peace may suddenly be broken. The cat peers warily from its mistress's side; the swords are close at hand.

The two of swords indicates a passionate and temperamental person who has been able to moderate his or her behavior through discipline and willpower. A stormy period in life may be passing. One may be called on to moderate a dispute or bring together antagonists.

Meanings: Balance through understanding. Peace. Calm. Familiarity. Harmony. Concord. Offsetting factors. Stalemate. Ambiguity. Vagueness. Contradictory thoughts. Duplicity. Lies.

THREE OF SWORDS

Three of Swords

Three people in black stand in a stone courtyard. A rose pierced by three swords is before them. Clouds darken the sky beyond.

The three figures preside at the destruction of the rose. A sense of ritual is given by their clothes and their rigid posture. The woman is completely covered, from head to toe, concealing whatever emotions she may feel at the vivisection of the flower.

The rose in Western culture is a symbol of emotional and physical passion. It is also to the West what the lotus is to the East: an emblem of spiritual unfoldment, of vulnerability.

When one opens one's heart, as a child or as an adult, and meets indifference, rejection, or exploitation, the wounds are deep. The pain can be so intense that rather than attempting to heal, one decides to cut away what is perceived as the source of pain: the heart itself.

The figures on the three of swords are victims as much as the rose. Contempt for the emotions, narrow-mindedness, and alienation from their fellows are the three swords they will use to amputate their own hearts. Love will be seen as sentimental treacle, religion as superstitious nonsense, expression of the emotions as weakness. They will convince themselves that

111

everyone is selfishly pursuing personal ends, and so the best they can do is win the competition. They may join a church or a political movement with the aim to stifle joy and freedom wherever these qualities may lurk.

Meanings: Lack of mercy. Separation. Alienation. Grief. Error. Absence. Sorrow. Locked-up emotions. Religious bigotry. Self-righteousness. Removal. Dispersion. Conscious insight. Decisive realization.

Four of Swords

Four of Swords

Four men rest at an oasis. Their swords lie on the carpet in front of them. The planet Jupiter, whose sigil is on the carpet, signifies expansion, understanding, philosophy, and law.

The four of swords does not show the kind of inner truce shown on the two of swords. The interval of peace here has been reached through negotiation and the agreement to follow rules. The four men reflect the ideal of human community, in which personal aims and conflicts are subjected to the good of society. If the men are usually adversaries, the influence of Jupiter gives them a way to lay down their swords without losing face.

The four of swords can also mean a rest or recovery from illness, respite at an oasis of calm after a harrowing journey through the desert.

Meanings: Truce. Alliance. Peace talks. Calm after a conflict. Interval. Retreat. Agreement. Concentration. Mental work.

Mental challenges. Respite. Rest after illness. Repose. Replenishment. Solitude. Exile.

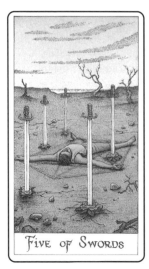

FIVE OF SWORDS

Five of Swords

A man lies on the ground, hemmed in by five swords that pierce roses. Around him is a wasteland; in the distance is the ocean. A pentagram encompasses his body; the five points and their connecting lines symbolize the five senses.

The swords pinning the roses indicate that mental processes have been used to enslave the passions and spirit. Perhaps at one time the man thought this would give him power; now his energy and will are sapped. Although the man is not actually pinned down by the swords, he is passive within their influence. The land around him shows only the skeleton of its former fruitfulness.

The five of swords indicates a quest for dominion that has ended in defeat. Humiliating as it might be, the only thing to do is to accept the situation. Time will bring a more useful perspective.

Meanings: Disgrace. Weakness. Blame. Late insight. Acceptance of the unavoidable. Clear perspective. New knowledge. Degradation. Adversary may arise. Infamy. Dishonor. Uncertain outlook.

Six of Swords

Six of Swords

A dancer poses on one foot. Behind him is a caduceus, near which is a pyramid. The highest discipline shows in the lines of the dancer's body. The swords pointing toward his foot admonish him to maintain perfect form.

Different spiritual leaders, for example, Rudolf Steiner and G.I. Gurdjieff, created body movements and postures intended to evoke specific states of mental awareness. Martial arts, such as tai chi and tae kwon do, use the body to enhance mental acuity, and the mind to enhance physical prowess and grace. Hatha yoga is a series of exercises that yoke together body and mind. The positions of ballet are intended to create an aesthetic effect on the beholder.

These arts are not creative. The forms are dictated by tradition and passed on by a living teacher, master, or guru. Their fruit are reaped only through dedication and regular practice.

The six of swords indicates that the rewards of discipline and hard work are beginning to manifest. The breakthrough may be in the healing arts, as indicated by the caduceus in the background, or in any field that emphasizes the connection of body and mind. A transition may be coming; during the change, help will come from a person whose self-discipline gives him or her a rather cold demeanor.

Meanings: Science. Deserved success. Balance. Intelligent behavior. Explanation. Change in the way of thinking. New mental orientation. Conscious association. A trip or journey.

Headstrong attempts to overcome difficulties. Expedient manner. Success after anxiety. Graduation from school.

SEVEN OF SWORDS

Seven of Swords

A woman walks into a hazy landscape. Swords are sunk in the ground around her. She is mostly covered by a large cloak.

Uncertainty pervades the card, from the cloud-swept moon to the cloaked figure. The woman walks barefoot in a field of blades and yet has an aura of carelessness.

Situations can reach a point where the only logical action seems to be to walk away from them. Before the first step is taken, though, one must examine one's motives. Is giving up merely the easy way out, an abdication of responsibility? Or is it the best way to cut losses? Will giving up on one approach open the way for another, or will it lead to yet another dead end?

The seven of swords indicates a situation that has become ambiguous at best. One must make a commitment or withdraw completely. Vagueness or inconsistency from self and others can be a source of frustration. An experienced person may be able to provide some direction.

Meanings: Uselessness. Vain effort. Inconstant behavior. Tolerance. Unclear intentions. Advice. New plans. Wishes. Consciously defining a goal.

Eight of Swords

Eight of Swords

A man and a woman stand in a pen of swords. A gray wall rises behind them. The ground is as uncertain as melting ice.

The grievances indicated by the eight swords are entrenched; neither the man nor the woman will make the first move toward resolution. They are no longer certain who is right and who is wrong, but pride or fear of losing control keeps them locked in the roles of adversaries.

The eight of swords indicates a conflict, internal or external, that both sides will lose unless some compromise or agreement is reached. Recriminations have decayed self-confidence and sympathy. The saving grace is that both sides are beginning to realize how much the situation has deteriorated. Neither can extricate himself or herself alone: it's all for one and one for all. Most likely, whoever takes the risk of making the first move will be met more than halfway.

Meanings: Disturbance. Interference. Limitation. Conflict. Blame. Resistance. Problematic thoughts. Mental prison. Imprisonment. Criticism. Limitation of ideas. Great mental tasks. Past treachery.

NINE OF SWORDS

Nine of Swords

War ravages a landscape. Swords fly through the air, striking an unarmed man. Another sword hits the serpent of life.

The nine of swords shows a man who is, or at least perceives himself to be, a victim of malice beyond his control. Whether his personal enemy or his country's enemy considers the attack to be just, it is he who must pay with his life.

Everyone, from the most macho man to the most protective parent, must face the fact that there are forces stronger than themselves. War, rape, epidemics, natural and ecological disasters, murder—these terrifying events sweep across gender, class, color, religion, and nationality. The highest religious and secular leaders have felt the assassin's bullet; palaces, temples, and hovels alike are flattened by bombs.

Protection is not found in ignorance or passivity. One must demand universal suffrage, full education for adults and children, a clean environment, safe housing and unbiased police protection, respect and opportunities regardless of color, gender, nationality, and sexual orientation. One cannot demand these rights for oneself only. History has made it clear that everyone must enjoy the same civil and human rights.

Another kind of war is waged within. Guilt, anxiety, hatred of self, conflicts between personal needs and the needs of others, depression, and worry about things that are out of one's power to change can gnaw away at self-esteem.

The nine of swords indicates an urgent need to assert control over negative forces, external and/or internal. Possibly one has been living in a cocoon, unaware of world events and unaware of one's own mental currents. It's time to come out, to take action and become involved. Constructive efforts will help.

Meanings: War. Despair. Sadness. Failure. Negative thoughts. Fear. Shame. Anxiety over a loved one. Acceptance of reality. Self-realization. Brilliant ideas.

TEN OF SWORDS

Ten of Swords

The ten of swords is the most frightening card of the Cosmic Tarot. It is an image of madness, a person besieged by the anguish of his own mind. The sun, far from being a healer, burns the sky into splinters.

Insanity has been perceived in many ways in different societies. Sometimes madness is considered divine; sometimes it is considered a curse. When severe mental illness strikes close to home, it is hard to see it as anything but a huge, painful puzzle that overwhelms our best intentions and most cherished ambitions. Only one thing seems really clear: the stable, functional mind is the most precious jewel we can ever have.

The urge to discredit those who are diagnosed as mentally ill, to dismiss them as "nuts," is a sign of the conformist in all of us. A patronizing attempt at pity can be a mask over the fear that is raised when basic assumptions about reality are questioned by "inappropriate" behavior and ideas.

The ten of swords warns of mental problems. The problem may be more or less intense; a sense of depression and anxiety could be a cloud in an otherwise sunny sky. More seriously, ideas can take on overwhelming or grandiose proportions; thoughts may be obsessive, confused, disconnected. A painful sense of distance from one's emotions might be experienced. Inescapable despair may lead to suicide fantasies or attempts.

Whether the problem is serious or mild, pay attention to it. Talk to someone who is stable, mature, and supportive. Browbeating yourself or turning up the pressure is no solution; be nurturing and gentle. If it is a friend or relative, or even a stranger on the street who is suffering, don't ignore the problem. Don't be afraid. Meet this person with all the compassion of your heart.

Meanings: Ruin. Destruction. Defeat. Mental confusion. Overwhelming thoughts. Pain. Mental anguish. The lowest point is reached. Acceptance of the unexpected. New mental horizons. Improvement. Help is on the way.

PRINCESS OF SWORDS

Princess of Swords

A woman is against the background of mountains and sky. Her companion is a hawk. A transparent sword rises from a flower.

The princess of swords wears the emblem of air, a triangle crossed with a hooked line. She operates in the realm of the mind, the intellect. Her gaze is direct, almost merciless; she is not inclined to compromise truth in order to spare the emotions of herself or others. Like the hawk who sees the tiniest creatures on the ground from high above, her mind misses nothing. The sword that rises from the lotus flower separates good from evil, truth from lies. Vagueness or compromise won't be allowed.

The princess of swords lives by her ideas and principles. She is a "stirrer-upper," an iconoclast. She may not have suffered enough in life to be merciful or tolerant of her elders' little weaknesses and hypocrisies. If dumb complacency sets in, the princess will be the one to uproot it. If there is a cause, the princess will be the firebrand at the lead, or the conspirator behind the scenes.

Because the princess expresses herself in action rather than words, she is a silent type. Her nature tends to draw secrets from people. In friendship, she is a reliable confidante; otherwise, she is an excellent spy or agent provocateur.

Meanings: Skill. Practical abilities. Observant. Powerful. Serious. Vigilance. Agility. Spying. A discreet person. An active youth. A person adept at perceiving, discerning, and uncovering the unknown or that which is less than obvious. Insight. Severity. Aggressiveness. An imposter revealed.

PRINCE OF SWORDS

Prince of Swords

A young man is in a lush landscape. A book and a sword, together with a lily, are before him. On his lapel is the sigil for air; on his cravat is the sigil for the astrological sign Aquarius. A hawk is behind his right shoulder.

The princess of swords was a woman of few words; the prince is "of the book." His philosophy has been worked out and formulated in elaborate terms, always subject to refinement and revision. He has his—and your—utopia all planned out. The thick book, however, cannot contain all his ideas. He is ready to talk to whomever will listen, perhaps beyond the limits of most people's endurance.

The expression of the prince is mild, but he is not an armchair philosopher. The sword is prominent. The prince's idealism can carry him into fanaticism, and conversion by the sword may seem to him the most expedient way to save the world.

Not all missionaries are bigoted, however, and the prince can be a true ambassador of good will. He genuinely enjoys sharing ideas and mingling with people of different cultures and kinds. The purpose of his travels will be to teach, rather than to convert; and to learn and absorb new outlooks, rather than to suppress others. He will be at home in multicultural institutes and ecumenical religious gatherings.

121

Though acting isn't necessarily a profession to which he would gravitate, the prince loves theatricality and eccentricity; he may have an unusual circle of friends. His noncomformist outlook can make him a true advocate of people who are alienated from the mainstream of society. Open-mindedness and an innate wish to help others give him the potential to be a valuable mental health worker, if he can learn to be more of a listener and less of a talker.

Unlike the Scorpian prince of cups, the prince of swords tends to love the world, rather than to focus on individuals. This makes him an ideal partner for free-spirited types who are normally suffocated in monogamous relationships. He is an excellent companion to "cerebral" types. He is stimulating intellectually, with the ability to make abstractions come alive. Ideas and more ideas flow from him; to expect realism and carefully laid plans is to miss a wonderful opportunity to explore new regions of the mind and the imagination.

To more down-to-earth people, the prince's carefully worked out and dazzlingly innovative philosophy may seem rather like a grab-bag of half-baked eccentricities. If there is a "New Age" type, it is the Aquarian prince of swords.

Meanings: Bravery. Agility. Cleverness. Swiftness. Foresight. Loyalty. Courage. Skill. Capacity. The strength and dash of a young man. Impetuous rush into the unknown without fear. Daring. Belligerent. Imprudence. Impulsive mistakes. Bigotry.

QUEEN OF SWORDS

Queen of Swords

A mature woman sits in a rich chamber, a sword in hand. A dove is in front of her. In the background is the couple from VI The Lovers. On the corners of the woman's cape are the sigils for the astrological sign Gemini and the element of water. At the top of her throne is the sigil for Mercury, ruler of Gemini. The eyes of the queen are her most outstanding feature: discerning, intelligent, not piercing but nevertheless intense.

Mercury was messenger to the Roman gods, and so Gemini (and Virgo, also ruled by Mercury) oversees writers, publishing and the printing industry, and communications. The medium of electricity is mercurial.

Like electrical current, the queen's mind moves quickly. What she says will be right to the point; aphorisms are more to her taste than philosophies. She may be an essayist or columnist; journalism that focuses on current issues is her forte. She delights in verbal sparring; some may find her argumentative. The satisfaction of producing a witticism means more to the queen of swords than having an idea adopted. Her interest in the water element indicates her realization that simple emotional gratification can go further with people than the most profound inspiration. The volatile, quick-tongued Cyrano de Bergerac demonstrates the Gemini temperament (augmented by an uncharacteristic fidelity), as does the loquacious, madcap Mercutio of Shakespeare's *Romeo and Juliet*.

The lovers in the background reflect the queen's role as a messenger, a medium that makes relationships possible. She may not be interested in maintaining a longterm relationship herself, but she loves matchmaking. She can be a delightful ally in a romantic intrigue; she may be a busybody.

The lovers can also be an image of happy days gone by. Sometimes the queen of swords signifies a person in mourning. The queen of swords could be someone whose responsibilities bar her or him from the garden of youth, someone who is temporarily separated from loved ones, or someone in exile.

The symbol of Gemini is twins, a dualism underlined by the presence of the Lovers. Gemini can run two operations simultaneously. The armed "peacekeeper" is one of the paradoxes of her realm.

Gemini rules the hands, and given the connection with electricity, the queen of swords loves gadgets, especially electronics and computers. Her mate, the Libran king of swords, and son, the Aquarian prince of swords, can have the software. The queen will tinker with the hardware. Space travel and all agencies connected with it are ruled by Gemini.

Meanings: Concentration. Severity. Grace. Attentiveness. Repartee. Quick wits. Intensely perceptive person. A subtle person. Mourning. Exile. Privation. Absence. Cunning. Cruelty. Narrow-mindedness. Maliciousness.

King of Swords

King of Swords

A man stands with sword and falcon in a temperate landscape. The sigil of Libra, which is ruled by Venus, is on his shirt. The king of swords, like the prince of swords, does not gaze directly toward the viewer. His eyes are lifted to the distance. His falcon, however, looks directly out, fully aware.

The king of swords rules through his intellect more than through physical might or emotional manipulation. He is keenly intelligent and can think quickly. Innate chivalry, dedication to his group, and mental prowess make him a good military commander, especially in a tactical capacity. He will competently organize a plan, and a group of people to execute it. His interests tend to shift quickly, and he is better at planning than following through. He can be a dilettante. His Venusian brother, the Taurean prince of pentacles, is the one for the longterm effort. The king's flitting attention is a paradox to his elephantine memory. He may avoid making enemies, but he can hold grudges against friends for a long, long time.

The king's devotion to mental activity often obscures other areas of his life. Ignoring emotions or physical desire doesn't make them go away, and the king may find that his loftiest ideas are actually the means to emotional or physical gratification. He is perceptive enough, usually, to catch himself; the slight uncertainty in his expression reveals that he never ceases reviewing his own motives or the motives of others.

The king's intuition is keen and his analyses are apt, and he knows it. If he happens to be wrong, his friends will find it very difficult to persuade him to see his error.

A harmonious society, a harmonious relationship is the chief desire of Libra. The distant gaze of the king reflects a wish for happiness beyond personal fulfillment. Venus rules him; love is the key to his great society.

The king of swords indicates a person who works ceaselessly for harmony, or at least an appearance of harmony. He is a good leader in a situation that requires a consensus. This is the diplomat, the emissary, the one who smoothes ruffled feathers. In a family, the king of swords is the one who holds the group together—the matriarch or patriarch of the clan or the child who takes on the role of peacemaker.

Meanings: Power. Daring. Authoritativeness. Sharp wits. Superiority. Reserved nature. Experienced person. Command of a situation. A professional. Highly analytical person. Justness. A person having many ideas, thoughts and designs. Stubbornness. Tyranny. A person who may pursue a matter to ruin. Sadism.

SUIT OF PENTACLES

ACE OF PENTACLES

Ace of Pentacles

A disk on which a pentacle is engraved stands among rocks on a plain. Crystals and bricks of gold are in front of it.

Earth, element of the suit of pentacles, is the seat of worldly wealth. Our food comes from the earth; gems and precious metals are mined from the depths. Although water dominates our bodies, we tend to think of ourselves as earthy. Symbolically, the element of earth is dense and heavy, retentive, and slow to change.

The ace of pentacles represents our material lives. The five points of the pentacle on the disk symbolize the five senses, the means by which we perceive and receive the world. The pentacle is the gateway to sensuous bliss and to an abyss of soul-deadening materialism. The disk itself is like a coin; physical sustenance must be paid for, with money and/or work. The crystals, harvested from the earth, are healing stones as well as prisms of that most elusive thing: light. The gold bricks pave the way to material comfort and generosity, as well as inspiring greed, stinginess, and jealousy.

The sense-driven body is often seen as an obstacle to spiritual realization, but our body is our vehicle, by grace or karma. Our senses can tune in the divine through incense, song, chanting, images of saints and deities, calligraphy, nature, the light around each other, and dance. The power of the physical dimension calls for discipline or, for many, denial.

Meanings: Wealth. Fertility. Dowry. Perfection. Personal talent. Personal task. Attainment. Prosperity. Felicity. Bliss. Gold. Treasures. Waste. Corruption by money. Miserliness. Greed. Fool's gold.

Two of Pentacles

Two of Pentacles

A youth dances barefoot in the sand, celebrating life. A boat with a yin-yang symbol on its sail is in the water behind the boy. A serpent is at his feet.

The snake has appeared in cultures as a symbol of evil and temptation, as well as of wisdom. Jesus said, "Be wise as serpents, and gentle as doves"; the devil took the guise of a serpent when he tempted Eve to eat of the Tree of Knowledge. Nagas, supernatural snakes, guard wisdom teachings in Asia; dragons, giant fire-breathing snakes, hoard huge Nordic stashes of gold, vaporizing anyone who takes even a penny's worth. These myths from different ends of the earth have in common the earth-dwelling snake as guardian of a treasure, spiritual or material, that can be won only by a virtuous and gifted person, one who is able to share with the community the riches gained.

The form of the boy's dance is echoed by the two pentacles on the dancer's shirt. Give and take, yin and yang, we share in dancing, in giving gifts, in teaching, in serving others, whether they are human, plant, or animal, in all sorts of ways that are, fortunately, accessible to all of us.

The two of coins brings opportunities for complementary "opposites" to meet: teacher with student, healer with diseased, parent with child, woman with man, need with income, patron with artist, boredom with exciting changes. Possibly, there will be a conflict of interests, causing some embarrassment and the need to reshuffle priorities.

Meanings: Changes. Attraction of opposites. Harmonious change. Cheerfulness. New complications. Excitement. News. Message or letter. Difficulty in launching new projects. Embarrassment. Contradictory changes. Contradictory tasks.

THREE OF PENTACLES

Three of Pentacles

Three men work on a stone building. A large window is designed with three pentacles. In the foreground is a blueprint and a compass.

If the two of pentacles brings about meetings of complementary types, the three of pentacles shows the housing of these meetings. It is like the first house of a couple, the work commissioned from an artist by a patron, the launch of a business by investor and manager. The plans have been made; now they are being carried out.

The initial stage is crucial to the ultimate outcome of any venture, be it romantic, artistic, or monetary. If the foundations are weak, if the materials used are shoddy, if the craftsmanship is poor, the entire edifice will be weakened and will not last long. If the foundations are sound, the materials carefully chosen, and the craftsmanship meticulous, the result will be pleasing and durable.

Obstacles may arise, but concerted effort can overcome them. It is vital at this point that everyone involved, from the janitor to the chairman of the board, from the apprentice to the journeyman, is concerned with the work, not only for its fruit, but for the process itself.

Meanings: Work. Material foundation. Effort. Reputation. Perseverance. Great skill in trade or work. Mastery. Perfection. Renown. Obstinacy. Fame. Narrow-mindedness. Weakness. Sloppiness. Mediocrity. Money problems. Commonplace ideas. Preoccupation.

FOUR OF PENTACLES

Four of Pentacles

A man sits in an easy chair. On the pocket of his jacket is a symbol of the sun. Behind him are books, a priceless vase, a telephone, and a tapestry. The tapestry is decorated with four pentacles and a sigil of the astrological sign Capricorn. In the background is a country mansion and a limousine. A woman stands before the man; she seems to be a petitioner.

The expression of the man is somber, but he relishes his prosperity. His intentions toward the woman may be beneficent, nevertheless his attitude is patronizing. He might be the

Important Executive, always busy, always preoccupied. This type makes clear to all who approach—including spouse and children—that only with great effort and generosity is he able to tear a bit of time from Important Business. Though wealthy, he is a miser; he has many "practical" reasons for not giving. He feels that he has a right to hang on to every penny of the money he has earned.

Alternatively, the man portrayed might represent a wealthy person whose generosity makes him vulnerable to solicitations. His generosity is measured and does not impinge on his personal wealth, but he is aware of the good he can do with his money. The four of pentacles can symbolize institutions, grants, trusts, scholarships, and foundations established by philanthropists.

The four of pentacles represents the accretion of wealth over time, through hard work and discipline. The wealth is usually material, but can also be in the form of power and influence. A tendency to hoard struggles against a basic sense that *noblesse oblige*.

Meanings: Power. Legacy. Gift. Great talent. Love of wealth. Wish to provide for others. Generosity. Application for a grant or scholarship. Hoarder. Usurer. Skinflint. Inability to share. Clinging to property. Avarice. Obstacles. Pride. Setbacks in business. Spendthrift.

FIVE OF PENTACLES

Five of Pentacles

Five bundled-up people walk through the rubble of war. The person with the basket is grimly intent on salvaging what can be saved from the ruins. The person behind, in the center, wears blankets in a form that is almost like a shell or an Egyptian mummy case. The figures in the background wander about empty-handed. The foremost one has an enigmatic expression; a smile touches the mouth, in spite of the surrounding devastation.

People react in different ways when confronted with ruin. Some get to work and try to make something of the wreckage, even if that thing is a poor shadow of what has been destroyed. Some retreat into their shells and wait with the thin hope that a savior will appear or that the situation will improve simply with the passage of time. Some give up and leave the situation entirely: rejecting responsibility or cutting losses. Sudden loss stuns many, rendering them unable to act, unable to make decisions, unable even to comprehend what has happened, how it came about.

The five of pentacles points to a situation that has deteriorated to the point of utter collapse. An immense effort must be made to start anew. It is counterproductive to beat oneself up for failing; reassessing possibilities and formulating a plan will bring recovery. Possibly, one will be called on to help someone who is down and out, whether or not one feels this person deserves help. Volunteer work might provide valuable contacts and a much-needed boost to self-esteem.

Meanings: Worry. Torture. Chaos. Poverty. Effort. Tension. Need. Loss. Failure. Error. Idleness. Immorality. Belief in the future. Reconciliation. Sharing one's last dime.

Six of Pentacles

Six of Pentacles

A man embraces six pentacles by the light of the crescent moon. He stands on a peak; in the distance are mountains and a lake.

Success is described in terms of heights and peaks and high points. The balance of the pentacles that arch over the moon indicates stability beyond change, beyond the phases of increase and decrease that are like the waxing and waning moon. The man is in the right place at the right time, and he is making the most of it.

The six of pentacles indicates having the means to be generous. This does not necessarily mean material wealth; generosity comes from the heart, not from the pocketbook. It is time to enjoy giving gifts and to share the fruits of hard work. Opportunities fall into one's hands like ripe plums.

Meanings: Success. Stability. Right timing. Scholarship or grant approved. Kindness. Generosity. Philanthropy. Charity. Gifts. Indulgence. Desire. Envy. Jealousy.

SEVEN OF PENTACLES

Seven of Pentacles

A man walks disconsolately through a region of distress. Broken and buried pentacles mean lost fortunes or inaccessible wealth. Vultures are perched on a tree in the background.

The seven of pentacles warns of a downturn in fortune. Hard work seems futile; setbacks come one after another; creditors are closing in like vultures. Possibly, circumstances have worked against us: we were laid off, the rent was raised, unexpected medical or legal expenses snatched savings away. Possibly, the trouble is due to mindless spending, lack of planning, and unrealistic, impulsive investments.

Concrete financial planning and discipline are essential. Maturity and a realistic outlook, and time and patience, will bring success or at least stability. One should review carefully one's assets—something might have been overlooked. Compassion for those who are worse off gives a sense of perspective.

Meanings: Failure. Bad business. Hard work with little success. Hazardous speculation. Bad investments. Ingenuity. Growth. Hard work begins to yield fruit. Inventiveness. Good business.

EIGHT OF PENTACLES

Eight of Pentacles

A woman gazes at a rose that is surrounded by eight pentacles and illuminated from above. The rose symbolizes human love: the passion of a lover, the loyalty of kinfolks, joy in the presence of friends, affection for animal companions, as well as compassion for all beings.

The eight of pentacles indicates the possibility of putting one's physical resources to the service of a higher cause. This can be in the form of a donation to charity, or it can be work for a cause. Cooking a meal for family and friends or for homeless folks, knitting a sweater for a soldier overseas or little caps for premature babies in hospitals, reclaiming wasteland with a garden for all to enjoy, making a toy for a child, being a buddy to an ill person are all ways in which we enjoy sharing our earthly resources. On the highest level, such work is done humbly, without the wish for return or reward. Generally, though, even the most modest person appreciates the gift of appreciation.

Meanings: Wisdom. Reason. Skill. Humility. Cleverness. Fulfilling work. Apprenticeship. Craftsmanship. Quickness to learn. Modesty. Ambition. Greed. Vanity.

NINE OF PENTACLES

Nine of Pentacles

A woman sits amidst riches, a key in her right hand. Coins come out of a treasure box.

The image framed by the window is a bit unreal. The house, the big car, the surrounding park, even the bird seem placed for effect. The accoutrements of wealth, which include, of course, a beautiful woman, are as if staged; one almost expects a voice-over extolling a brand of wine or the powerful motor of the car.

The woman holds the key to the scene. If she is imprisoned by her wealth, she also has the means to be released from it. It is she who has set the scene, and she can let down the curtain any time she wishes. The nine of pentacles can indicate control over one's circumstances, but it can also hint at a feeling of being a spectator to one's own life.

The nine of pentacles indicates a dynamic person who has the ability to stage scenes, to make things happen. Part of this person's power may derive from material wealth. Mostly, however, imagination and the knack of getting other people to do the "donkey work" make this person the calm and collected center of a self-created world. She is terrific at organizing large groups of people à la Cecil B. De Mille. Operatic works, glitzy charity balls, lavish weddings, haute couture fashion shows, huge conventions, film or stage productions with enormous casts and ever-changing sets: she can handle them.

Meanings: Gain. Growth. Popularity. Property. Abundance.

Material wealth. Setting trends. Backstage life. Organizing spectacles. Material well-being. Waste. Diversion. Roguery. Possible loss of a valued friendship or a treasured possession.

TEN OF PENTACLES

Ten of Pentacles

A luxuriously dressed young man holds a white bird in his hand. In spite of his palatial surroundings, the youth looks pensive, almost sad.

The youth on the ten of pentacles savors a romantic Weltschmerz, world weariness, from a surfeit of riches. Everything has been given him, but it isn't enough. The young man cradles a bird near his heart. Perhaps he feels like a bird in an elegant cage. He may be unsure of whether he would even be able to fly, should he liberate himself.

The ten of pentacles illustrates an experience that each of us has at least once in life: reaching a pinnacle of complete success and recognition. We may receive an honor, an award, a degree, a promotion; our work is published or exhibited; a courtship culminates at our own spectacular wedding. Unexpectedly, though, the happiness at the peak is mixed with a feeling of emptiness. The prize is in our hand, but in a corner of ourselves, we are sad and perplexed. We may have the feeling of standing still while the world rushes on past us.

Contentment can avoid apathy and ennui if it is sparked with the inspiration to understand and carry out the demands of our innate capabilities. A surfeit of riches or success can instigate soul-searching and provide direction for more meaningful activity.

The ten of pentacles indicates talents waiting to be used. The potential to create, to build, is ripe; all the necessary abilities are in place. A supportive network of friends and relatives is ready to help. The young man on the ten of pentacles may be someone who is about to venture into the world, his confidence bolstered by the loving pride of his family. The capital necessary for a new venture is likely to materialize. If success has been met, enjoy—and move on to the next project.

Meanings: Security. Happiness. Developed talents. Lively habits. Riches. Safety. Family matters. Ancestry. Inheritance. Home. Venture. Danger. Bad odds. Possible loss. Robbery. Loss of inheritance. Dissipation. Gambling.

PRINCESS OF PENTACLES

Princess of Pentacles

The princess exists in a beautiful landscape of rock formations, waterfalls, and flowers. She wears a pentacle on her gown.

The princess of pentacles is very much of the earth realm. Comfort, sensual pleasure, material wealth are some of the things that make her happy. Earth inclinations can bring about greed, but usually the princess will fulfill herself through down-to-earth plans followed by hard, practical work. Because of her sincere involvement in labor, the princess is good at supervising others, able to give orders without being tyrannical or partial. She is not exceedingly proud, but since she is sensitive to the prestige of others, she is not likely to cause others to lose face. Corporate politics are to her an exasperating distraction from the job at hand.

Concern with material wealth can make the princess of coins the ultimate capitalist or the ultimate communist—both opposite sides of the same coin. The system of access to material wealth is, in her eyes, the determining factor in social health. If she is a scholarly type, she will devote herself to economics—probably conservative, possibly progressive. She may have a deep commitment to fair use of land resources or to alleviation of hunger. On the other hand, she could have a deep commitment to preserving wealth for her class or family, or merely for herself, regardless of moral or global considerations.

The princess of pentacles may be a sculptor, especially one who works with stone or metal, a potter, a smith or jeweller, or someone involved in the mineral fuels industries.

Meanings: Young, strong, promising person. Carefulness. Communication. Deep concentration and application. Scholarship. A do-gooder. Fondness of luxury. Spoiled person. Failure to recognize obvious facts. Illogical thinking. Wastefulness.

PRINCE OF PENTACLES

Prince of Pentacles

The prince is a confident young man wearing luxurious clothes. The banner and fence behind him give the impression of a military camp, as do the epaulets and cuffs of his jacket. The banner is topped with the symbol of Venus; on a cliff is a bull, symbol of Taurus.

Taurus is the most luxury-loving sign of the zodiac, and is especially drawn to the treasures of the earth: gems and minerals. The prince of pentacles can be ostentatious, as he is fascinated by "all that glitters." Pleasures of the body can also ensnare Taurus, who is ruled by Venus.

The earthy nature of the Taurean bull is reflected in deep-rooted loyalties to people and to place. Taurus does not delight in belligerence, but he will fight to preserve the religion, homeland, and customs of his clan. A firm sense of rightness can make him immovable. The prince's arms crossed over his chest, together with his narrowed eyes, give the impression that, like the bull, he will hold his ground.

The prince of pentacles reflects a militant stand on issues of homeland, the rights of indigenous peoples, access to natural resources, ecology. The organization Greenpeace is a prince of pentacles manifestation, as are those on the other side of the coin, industrialists who believe that society benefits from the exploitation of earth's resources, regardless of ecological ramifications. Struggles between ethnic groups for tracts of land are prince of pentacles dilemmas.

The prince of pentacles is a good person to have as an ally.

Once his loyalty is established, only blatant betrayal will uproot it. He is generous to friends and family, giving his wealth, time, and emotional support.

If there is a problem, the prince of pentacles will patiently and methodically work until a solution is reached, no matter how long it takes. His deliberateness and innate caution may lead others to consider him stupid. Dullness can be a trait of the prince, but more likely his wheels are turning efficiently behind an impassive facade.

The prince of pentacles is probably the worst person to have as an enemy. The vendetta may have been invented by him; time is no barrier to the prince's revenge. A tendency to perceive outsiders as enemies may cause problems, but as this tendency is rooted in an excess of loyalty rather than in paranoia it can be ameliorated with reason. The Libran king of swords, a fellow Venusian with a lighter touch, is the one to soften the Taurean prince of pentacles.

Meanings: Persistence. Inventiveness. Reliability. Readiness to help. Solidness. A true friend. Methodicalness. Pensiveness. Practicality. Patience. Ability to conclude a task. Laboriousness. Indolence. Stubbornness. Apathy. Mercilessness. Narrow-mindedness. Limits set by dogmatic views.

QUEEN OF PENTACLES

Queen of Pentacles

A serene woman is before her palace at the border of a lake. The flower holds a pentacle. The ear of wheat next to the pentacle is symbolic of Virgo, whose house rules harvest. The peak of the building behind the queen is topped with the sigil for Virgo.

The queen of pentacles is the essence of domestic well-being: good food, beautiful surroundings, repose, friendship, and love. She radiates a sense of composure, of quiet magnificence, of settled comfort. Originality is not her interest; she is for tradition. She craves fine things, both for status and for their intrinsic value. If her home is less than a palace, it may cramp her style, but she will find a way to make it inviting and gracious.

Because she cannot bear shabbiness, poverty, or mediocrity in her life, the queen of pentacles may indulge in shady business practices, persuading herself that the benefits she reaps will cause no harm to others. Speculation and get-rich-quick schemes are not for her, but with much logical and profit-oriented persuasion, she will back an innovative project. She may be a Robin Hood type, bending the rules to make sure all her dependents have enough on their plates.

The queen of pentacles indicates a person who is mature and prosperous. Food is one of her major interests; she may be a stay-at-home type whose kitchen always smells of delicious food, which can be sinfully rich or of the earthy "health nut" variety. She is inclined to be plump, unless she is into special diets such as macrobiotics. She is least likely to be seen at an aerobics class, except after big eating holidays. Her interests lie in nonindustrial crafts that are traditionally in the domain of women: quilting, weaving, embroidery, basketry, hand-built pottery, knitting, and decorating. She has a strong sense of color and visual harmony, and could be a painter who favors landscapes, still lifes, or bold abstracts. She is also quite at home with books, and may be a librarian or archivist.

Like the Gemini queen of swords, the Virgo queen is ruled by Mercury the messenger. Her facility at communication, her diligence, and her attention to order and detail make her an ideal secretary on a clerical or diplomatic level. She is also an excellent translator or interpreter.

In the home and on the job, the queen of pentacles is the one everyone turns to with their troubles as well as their joys. She tends not to confide her own problems unless she is truly desperate, so it is important that her friends and family not forget her needs as she cares for theirs. The queen of pentacles may appear as a beloved companion in cat form. A sleek, well-fed cat giving itself a good washing, from ears to toes, is a reflection of the fastidious and perfectionist queen of pentacles.

Meanings: Good-heartedness. Gentleness. Quiet. Benevolence. Friendliness. Riches. Zeal. Domesticity. Effort. Roots. Prosperity and well-being. Opulence. Generosity. Liberty. Magnificence. Dignity. A noble soul. Submissiveness. Impersonal attitude. Phlegmatic person.

King of Pentacles

King of Pentacles

The king of pentacles sits in an opulent room. He handles two gold coins. In the background is a goat, symbol of Capricorn.

As partner to the queen of pentacles, the king has a keen interest in business, as well as in legacies, trusts, inheritances, investments—anything that concerns money. He is not necessarily greedy. He considers himself a realist. From his perspective, money is the oil of society, capable of bestowing benefit or harm, depending on its use. He is well aware of status and the rewards it can bring in terms of power and favors. The king of pentacles is an ideal capitalist, balancing profit motive with paternalistic concern toward employees.

The king enjoys being surrounded by the signs of his success, but he buys only what he can afford. He can put up a good show on a poor pocketbook, as he is good at finding bargains and making deals. Credit does not appeal to him, unless he is the one collecting the interest.

The worry under the smile denotes an attitude that less somber personalities consider pessimistic. The king of pentacles lives under the conviction that one must be prepared for hard times. His first priority is security for self and others. Like the queen of pentacles, the king loves his food, and his chief physical pitfall is a tendency to hoard food in his own body—to be fat.

Outwardly impatient with foolish expenditures, Capricorn vicariously enjoys the extravagance of others. He values beautiful objects of lasting quality, especially as gifts, since he tends not to spend money on himself. Under a rather miserly exterior, Capricorn has a yielding heart. He will grumble his way to the ends of the earth to help someone in need.

The king's business and domestic life can be complicated by people giving and getting favors, but he basically prefers a simple life that revolves around work and family. Loved ones may chafe under his wish to control situations and relationships, and he may have a stormy relationship with his volatile son, the Taurean prince of pentacles. The king of pentacles is faithful as a spouse, business partner, or friend, and he expects others to be as committed as himself. If one word can describe the king, it is responsible. He is the pillar of strength in his clan.

Meanings: Diligence. Patience. Talent in mathematics. Wealth. Prudence. Tenderness. Epicureanism. Responsible person. Character and intelligence. Business acumen. Loyal friend. Reliable marriage partner. Wise investment. Ability to acquire money and valuable possessions. Greed. Corruption. Using any means to achieve the desired end. Thriftlessness.

• Using the Cosmic Tarot •

MOST PEOPLE CONSIDER THE TAROT TO BE A TOOL for divination, and many books offer excellent spreads for this purpose. But divination is only one way in which the tarot can be used. Contemplation of single cards can yield insights into the symbolic values of the cards, which can be applied to dream analysis, meditation, and the arts. One can use the cards to inspire one's own artistic renderings or imaginings. Many people use the tarot as a guide in studies of the Cabala, psychology, religion, alchemy, numerology, and so on.

This chapter offers divinatory spreads as well as activities that can enhance understanding of the tarot cards and of oneself. The emphasis is on interaction with the tarot, as opposed to passive acceptance of readings.

Considerations on Reading the Cards

> Genuine divination is a service performed in the temple of Truth. (Oswald Wirth, *Introduction to the Study of the Tarot*)

What does it mean, to be truthful? As social beings, most of us juggle truthfulness with self-protection and consideration for others. Sometimes it is difficult to draw the line between hypocrisy and being decent to people. We smile to ingratiate ourselves with others, to conceal pain from our children or from people who might worry if we are unhappy, to conceal vulnerability. Sometimes we conceal the truth: the timing is not right; the area is too sensitive; our truth is not relevant to the situation; we sense the truth is only relative to our own preconceptions or culture; or we simply don't have the courage to come out with the truth.

Each person has their own measure of honesty and their code of behavior vis-a-vis being truthful and being tactful. What seems to be fairly universal, though, is understanding that the path to the human heart is sincerity and trust, not brutal bluntness. As Norbert Lösche wrote in the booklet accompanying the Cosmic Tarot, "As you look inside yourself, remember that whatever lies close to your heart should be handled not only seriously, but also lovingly."

A cardreader touches issues of the human heart; sensitivity is essential to a reading that is honest, but not destructive of confidence and peace of mind. The drama of the images in a card spread can have great impact; the most rational, scientific types can be terrified by cards like Death or The Tower. If you do a reading for yourself, be aware of your mood, of your vulnerabilities. Never let someone persuade you to read their cards when your instinct resists, and be very careful about reading cards for people who are superstitious or suggestible. A cardreader might feel that the reading ends when the cards are returned to the stack, but many people remember and mull over a reading for a long, long time.

Honest awareness of one's own weaknesses is helpful. If the querent's expectations and desires are intimidating, we might be tempted to contrive an air of authoritativeness and omniscience. Perhaps we want to impress others through our knowledge of the cards or through psychic powers we claim to possess. We should acknowledge these temptations, and not base readings on them.

Most of us are unable to access psychic powers consistently and accurately; most of us are not trained psychotherapists; only the highest saints and sages have total insight. A Buddhist story relates that a man walking along the edge of a pond found a fish that had flipped itself out of the water. His compassion was aroused by its struggles, and he took it by the tail and flung it back in. The fish promptly ate the rest of the creatures in the pond. We are like the man: we want to do the right thing, but we don't have the ability to see the complete outcome.

A cardreader can't pretend to be a prophet or psychoanalyst; the vast majority of us have no training to counsel or assist people with serious problems. If someone seems to be deeply troubled, don't try to be a Mr. or Ms. Fix-it. Be ready to guide him or her to a professional counselor, a doctor or healer, or a community agency or support network.

This is not to say that we should be frozen into passivity, never helping, never hurting. However, we should always be flexible in reading the tarot, and we should impress this flexibility on anyone receiving a reading. The cards can offer insight into human nature, hints at possible courses of action, clues to obstacles or opportunities. Nevertheless, they are only images on paper, not commandments written in stone. Circumstances are mutable. The negative indicators that surface in most readings can help us face up to bad situations and patterns of negative thinking; they aren't character assessments or prophecies of doom and gloom. All factors, negative and positive, in a reading point to possibilities and tendencies, not fated events and hopelessly ingrained character traits.

So many disclaimers. . . . But so many people have been haunted for years by fairground palmists' or cardreaders' dire predictions, which are made with about as much thought and creativity as an assembly-line worker applies on the job. So many people waste hard-earned money on "spiritual advice"—which often centers on money or romantic manipulations, and is just food for fantasy. So many people mock the tarot because of the absurd presumptuousness and pretensions of readers who climb onto the pedestal of psychic, prophet, and know-it-all.

The images of the tarot can spark imaginative and rational faculties, and thus reinforce a feeling of control in our lives. A good reading gives a person something to work with, something that is real and in the present. The best readings are those to which the querent contributes, sometimes with a gratifying, "Aha! I knew that all along, but I couldn't put my finger on it!" The tarot points to the truth that is waiting to be discovered in each person. The temple of truth in which a reading should take place is not a palace built by the reader. It is a living creation of the reader and the querent.

Preparation

Rituals may or may not have innate power or results. At the very least, they serve to focus the mind. Short prayers, incantations, mantras, or meditative silence are useful to some readers. Others prefer to plunge straight into a reading because rituals baffle their concentration on the cards themselves. The environment is also your choice. Some people read best in a totally silent room; some do terrific readings in tearooms, bookstores, and even amidst the nightlife on the sidewalks of Greenwich Village in New York City. The universal preparation for a reading is the adoption of a serious (but not grim) attitude, an open mind, and a sensitive heart.

Before handling the cards, you should ask the querent or yourself if a particular question or issue is of concern. Usually people know exactly what they want to know, but they may be reluctant to reveal their secret worries. This is no problem. If you don't receive a specific question, you can do a general reading. Trust is built between the reader and the querent in the course of the reading, and the matter of concern will surface.

The mode of shuffling varies. You can riffle the cards, mix them hand over hand, put them down on the table and stir them up. You can cut them with your right hand or your left hand, seven times, three times, or just once (but do cut them, since the bottom card has a tendency to peak out during shuffling). As long as the cards are thoroughly mixed, the methods of mixing and cutting aren't important—unless you want to adopt a ritual.

Some readers ask the person receiving a reading to mix the cards, some ask the querent merely to cut the mixed cards. Some people wouldn't dream of letting others touch their deck under any circumstances, because the "vibrations" might be upset. Even the method of laying out the cards can vary. Most readers deal the cards themselves, with the top card going in the first position, next card in position two, and so on.

Once the cards are laid out, you can turn them all over and proceed with the reading, or you can read each card as you turn it over. You can do a brief reading of each card as it is turned over, and then do a more in-depth reading of the spread as a whole.

Divination begins before the cards are even shuffled. A person reveals much simply by voice, clothes, gait, expression, makeup or lack of makeup, and so on. While first impressions can be misleading, no more than a reflection of prejudices or stereotypes, thoughtful observations can help.

A trick of fortunetellers is to ask a seemingly trivial question, such as where a client got an article of her/his clothing, in order to elicit personal information and obtain a more "accurate" reading. Don't be tricky. If you want information about the querent, be up front and ask them what you need to know.

Relaxed concentration is the state of mind most conducive for reading the tarot. Keep the mind on the cards, but don't make it so tight that intuition is strangled. The traditional meanings of the cards have the authority of authentic symbolic values and long use. By bearing them in mind, one can be more objective, not captured by personal prejudices or by preconceptions concerning the querent. Traditional meanings need not be interpreted in a narrow or stereotyped way, however. The word "partnership," for example, calls up romance, business, and astrological configurations of the planets. Let your imagination range over the images; let your imagination blend with the thought of past men and women who have contributed to the resources of the tarot.

The Story Told by the Tarot

The cards are laid, the spread complete. The beginner sees a bewildering array of images, some contradictory, some vaguely similar, some frightening, some soothing. The experienced reader sees symbolic pictures of people, events, and influences which interact with each other as they move through time. In other words, the experienced reader sees a story. In tracing the story told by a spread, it helps to find a beginning, middle, and end, and events and characters.

The beginning of a reading can be considered the question asked by the querent. If no question is formulated, you could consider the beginning of the story to be the attitude, mood, or circumstances of the person receiving the reading. The beginning can also be the first card. The middle is the rest of the cards, up to the last one, which is usually an outcome card.

Most tarot spreads imply a flow of time. The past (the beginning) may be the immediate past or one's childhood. The present (the middle) is the here and now, or the present may be considered the time period in which the question at hand began to manifest. The future (the end) can indicate what is to come, a possible course of action one may wish to take in the future, or influences that bear on the future.

Any card in the tarot deck can symbolize a person, an event, an object, or a psychological issue: family, friend, employer or employee, colleague, social group, teacher, animal, a stranger who may have an impact on the situation, celebrities; a birth or death, a promotion, a meeting; buildings, institutions, dwellings,

The Cosmic Tarot

nations, cities, outdoor places, cultural events, a car; personal strengths and weaknesses, romantic interests, religious outlooks, behavioral patterns—the list is limitless.

The meanings of each card depend on the flow of the reading—that is, the cards that precede and follow the specific card being interpreted. The position of the card in the spread is also a deciding factor. Every single card relates to every other card in a spread. Sometimes it is helpful to move temporarily a card from its place in the spread and put it next to a card that seems strongly linked to it, and study the two cards as a pair.

Major Arcana cards do not dominate Minor Arcana cards; courts do not dominate numbered cards. All the cards work together. Occasionally, a single card or a few cards will seem to have more emphasis, a situation worth studying.

The cards in a reading are a story, a continuum. A configuration of, say, ten of swords, The Empress, and two of cups might mean that a motherly person (The Empress) will alleviate a personal disaster (ten of swords) by matching the querent with a partner, a lover, or a friend (two of cups). Or it could be that this motherly person is causing trouble in a relationship. Cards often have contradictory meanings; a wide range of interpretation gives the reader more freedom to "see" the individual's story.

The Time Spread

The Time Spread is specifically for beginners since it uses only four cards and deals with an obvious sequence of time. More experienced readers might like to use it as a quick and simple spread.

The reader should have a clear question in mind. While the question need not be a yes-or-no query, it should be specific and uncomplicated. Remember that the cards can refer to people or events.

Card 1: **The past** What led up to the present situation. This can refer to people or events of one's childhood, but more likely points to the events or people directly concerned with the situation.

Card 2: **The present** The way the situation stands at the moment.

Card 3: **The future** The likely outcome of the situation as manifested in the near future (within one or two months), if influences continue as expected.

Card 4: **Action** What one can do either to encourage the outcome or to change it—the querent chooses the way in which this card is to be used.

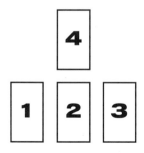

The Cosmic Tarot

The Cosmic Pentagram Spread

The design of the Cosmic Pentagram Spread is based on the pentagram and rose on the back of the Cosmic Tarot cards.

The first five cards are laid out in the same order one would use in drawing a five-pointed star, or a pentagram.

Card 1: **Intention** The Intention card clarifies the issue of the reading. It states our intention, the way in which we would like to see the situation in question resolved.

Card 2: **External Influences** This card reveals the powers that have led to the situation. The focus is on circumstances or people that we feel rule us or the situation. Possibly childhood events or events of the past may be of concern.

Card 3: **Hope** The Hope card reflects personal hopes.

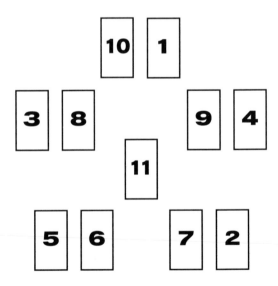

Card 4: **Fear** The Fear card reflects personal fears.

Card 5: **Internal Influences** This card reveals the factors of our personality that have created the situation. The focus is on inclinations, habits, and patterns of behavior.

The next five cards are laid out from the "feet" of the star to the "head."

Card 6: **Inner Will** Paired with card 5 Internal Influences, card 6 reveals sources of strength and insight.

Card 7: **Action** Paired with card 2 External Influences, card 7 indicates what action we can take.

Card 8: **Help** Paired with card 3 Hope, card 8 reveals factors that can be of assistance to us in the situation.

Card 9: **Obstacles** Paired with card 4 Fear, card 9 indicates inner blocks, sometimes perceived as external obstacles, that prevent the situation from being resolved favorably.

Card 10: **Aspirations** Card 10 takes us beyond the intention shown in card 1, beyond immediate needs and greeds. Now that the situation has been analyzed through the reading, we may have a more open mind about what we can accomplish.

Card 11: **Outcome** Card 11, in the center, shows the result of the factors indicated by all the other cards. The last card is a scenario that has been generated by the possibilities shown in the rest of the spread.

The Outcome card should be viewed in context with the Intention card as well as with the Aspiration card. If the Outcome is unfavorable, conflict among these three cards may give clues to the source of the problem. The Obstacles card can also offer clues.

The Human Community Spread

The Human Community Spread is unique in that it is dealt from a face up deck; the querent chooses the cards. It is for analyzing a social situation—a conflict, an election, new developments in science, the arts, or technology—but it is also useful in examining personal matters. The readings can focus on one's own region or on foreign places. If the spread is applied to a social situation, one generally reads for oneself, and is both reader and querent. Otherwise, the reading can be done for another person.

The deck should be well shuffled. A question must be stated in specific terms.

The reader turns the deck face up, and lays the cards down one by one in a single stack. A card should be laid down at about the rate of one every second. The querent should gaze with concentration at the cards as they are laid down.

The reader will then ask a series of ten questions. After each question is asked, the cards are laid down again, one at a time in a single stack, at the rate of one card every few seconds. When the querent spots a card that answers the question, he or she tells the reader to stop. The card is drawn out and put down face up; all ten cards will form a simple vertical line, with card 1 at the bottom, and card 10 at the top. If the querent was unable to select a card, lay down the deck one more time. (The deck does not need to be shuffled after each question.)

Card 1 What do you see as the heart of the present situation?

Card 2 What historical (childhood or long-term past) events led up to the current situation?

Card 3 What historical (childhood or long-term past) person or people led up to the current situation?

Card 4 What recent events led up to the current situation?

Card 5 What living person or group instigated the current situation?

Card 6 What is the most positive element in the situation?

Card 7 What is the most negative element in the situation?

Card 8 What kind of person can make the situation as positive as it can be?

Card 9 What action can most improve the situation?

Card 10 What is the likely outcome?

The Human Community Spread is not meant to be predictive. It helps us to articulate the way in which we relate to the world by clarifying our feelings and thoughts about issues. Readings of this kind can, over time, expose prejudices and ideals, fears and hopes. We may see a tendency to scapegoat or idealize a particular group or ideology; we may arrive at a more definite knowledge of the role we'd like to play in the world.

One may prefer doing a slower, more thoughtful reading of the Human Community Spread, especially if one is unfamiliar with tarot cards or with this particular deck. However, by viewing the cards rapidly, one is likely to be honest, not choosing the cards that support a self-image or that say what one wants to believe.

An Improvisation

In theater, improvisation is done by actors in order to explore characters, to loosen their imaginations as well as their bodies and voices, and to get to know each other. Generally, there are no sets or costumes, and there is no script. A scenario is chosen by a director, and the actors spontaneously create action and dialogue based on the scenario.

An Improvisation using the tarot is much like a theatrical

improvisation, except that we have the benefit of costumes and sets, courtesy of the images on the card. Anyone can play any character that appears on the cards: men can play women, women can play men; conservatives can be liberal, free spirits can be straight-laced. A theater troupe could use an Improvisation to help shape a performance piece. An Improvisation could also be useful in a class on tarot.

An Improvisation can be used to approach a personal problem, to explore a fantasy, to attempt to understand a situation in the world or in your social group. Scenarios can revolve around historical events, exotic travel fantasies, mysteries, surreal dream voyages.

Interpersonal relationships should be tackled only with people who have a relationship of trust. Possibly, a grudge can be aired or a quarrel patched up through an Improvisation, but no one should be embarrassed or harassed; personal secrets need not be aired. An Improvisation is not for deciding who's "right" and who's "wrong," but for exploration. As in any reading, everyone taking part should be sensitive to changes of mood that may take place as the reading unfolds.

An Improvisation can be done with any number of people, up to about eight. To begin, sit in a circle. Then choose a leader, either by drawing lots or by consensus. (The role of leader will revolve around the circle, with a new leader for each Improvisation.) The leader decides on the scenario for the Improvisation and also makes sure the Improvisation doesn't get out of hand. An Improvisation that goes on longer than ten or fifteen minutes tends to wander, and the leader should bring it to a close at that time, unless the group is very keen on continuing.

Shuffle the deck well. The leader draws the first card and suggests a scenario based on its image. The leader's card will determine the setting of the situation, and the leader will play the character presented on that card. The others in the group each draw a card in turn, starting from the person on the leader's right and moving round the circle. The card each person draws will decide his or her character, in terms of personality, inclinations, secret or overt agenda, and even physical appearance.

Members of an uninhibited group can act out the scenario themselves, or the group can use the cards as puppets. People may be shy or uncertain in the beginning; the leader should try to make sure everyone is included in the Improvisation, and that no one person dominates. With time, the group will warm up and gain confidence, and the improvisations will become more interesting.

An example of an Improvisation is:

Scenario: III The Empress A wealthy woman is sitting in her garden, where a party is taking place, and a bird flies up to her with a ruby in its beak.

Character 1: Eight of swords A woman who feels trapped in an unhappy marriage perceives the Empress as someone who's always had everything handed to her on a silver platter. The ruby confirms this feeling.

Character 2: Queen of pentacles She claims the ruby is hers.

Character 3: Two of wands This gentleman is courting the Empress. The woman on the eight of swords is smitten with him.

Character 4: Wheel of Fortune He is a compulsive gambler with some heavy debts to pay. The ruby could help him out.

The Cosmic Chain

The Cosmic Chain is similar to An Improvisation in that it is a creative group activity, and an amusing game. It is based on the genre of "chain poetry," in which a poem is written by a group, with each person writing a line. Four or five people comprise the ideal group for the Cosmic Chain. You will need a pad of paper and a pen, in addition to the deck.

Everyone should sit in a circle, with the deck in the center. The deck is shuffled well, and the first person (chosen by lot or consensus) draws a card. He or she writes a line of poetry based on the image on the card. The card is placed face up to the right of the deck. The pad and pen are passed to the next person, who draws another card from the deck, writes a line of poetry, and places the drawn card to the right of the other face-up card—and so on, around the circle. Pass the paper and pen around until the poem reaches about twenty-five lines. Everyone should write an equal number of lines. The last person to draw will read the poem aloud, holding up for everyone to see the card that corresponds to each line.

The poem does not have to be deep and clever, nor does it have to rhyme. It will likely range from hilarious to contemplative. An interesting experiment is to have each person write "blind," that is, without seeing what anyone else has written, working only from the laid-out cards. Also, you can write a story or drama instead of a poem, or you can focus the work on a certain subject. Like An Improvisation, the Cosmic Chain can be helpful to a tarot class, or to any group of people who want fresh ideas on the tarot, or any other subject.

• Annotated Bibliography •

Calvino, Italo. *The Castle of Crossed Destinies.* New York: Harcourt Brace Jovanovich, 1969. Calvino's magical book is about men and women, strangers and travelers, who meet in a mysterious castle in a huge forest. They find themselves mute but itching to tell the stories of their journeys. They use tarot cards. Besides being enormously amusing, the stories provide excellent examples in how to see the tarot cards as a flow of narrative. To add to the fun, Calvino presents various, sometimes conflicting accounts for each storybook spread of cards.

Clarson, Laura E. *Tarot Unveiled: The Method to Its Magic.* Stamford, Conn.: U.S. Games Systems, 1988. *Tarot Unveiled* is simply about how to read tarot cards—no esoteric symbolism, no complicated psychology or mysticism. Included is a chapter "The Ethics of Reading for Others." Illustrated with the Hanson-Roberts Tarot deck.

Kaplan, Stuart R. *The Encyclopedia of Tarot.* Volumes I (1978), II (1986), and III (1990). Stamford, Conn.: U.S. Games Systems. The Encyclopedias open up a world of tarot decks. The decks described and illustrated date from the Italian Renaissance to the present, and cover every political, personal, cultural, and religious interest under the sun—from teddy bears to Victoriana, to human anatomy, to Sufism, to comedy, to cats. Some of the decks are naive, but poignant; many show real artistic finesse. Besides the pictures, the books offer a history of the tarot, an analysis of its symbolism, and chapters on figures such as Pamela Colman Smith, artist of the Rider-Waite Tarot deck, and the Visconti and Sforza families of Milan, who commissioned the earliest extant tarot decks.

The Cosmic Tarot

Oken, Alan. *Alan Oken's Complete Astrology.* New York: Bantam Books, 1980. A well-written and organized book that covers the mythological, spiritual, and mundane aspects of astrology.

von Rohr, Wulfing, and Gayan S. Winter. *Tarot of Love.* Stamford, Conn., 1992. U.S. Games Systems. *Tarot of Love,* companion to the deck of the same name, applies the tarot to the realm of personal relationships. Family, lovers, and friends are the focus. The book has a modern psychotherapeutic outlook, but is not bogged down in jargon and "correct" models of behavior. Tarot of Love is very here and now. It will bring fresh air into your relationships.

Williams, Brian. *A Renaissance Tarot.* Stamford, Conn., 1993. U.S. Games Systems. The companion book to the beautiful Renaissance Tarot deck presents a lucid and graceful intertwining of classical, medieval, and Renaissance influences on the tarot. Williams' knowledge of art history, iconography, and mythology brings to life the symbols of the tarot. To this he adds his own wisdom, the wisdom of sages such as William Shakespeare, and folk wisdom in the form of proverbs. A special feature of the book is the author's line-drawing reproductions of classical, medieval, and Renaissance art.

Wirth, Oswald. *Introduction to the Study of Tarot.* With a foreword by Stuart R. Kaplan. 1983, Stamford, Conn. U.S. Games Systems. This accessible, brief book provides a good approach to using the tarot imaginatively while respecting its traditions.

Wirth, Oswald. *The Tarot of the Magicians.* (Translation of *Le Tarot, les imagiers du Moyen Age.*) 1985, York Beach, Maine. Samuel Weiser. Wirth's book is an unpretentious description of the esoteric tarot, with interpretations of alchemical, Rosicrucian, Cabalistic, Masonic, and astrological symbolism. The illustrations and diagrams are elegant.

Thank you ...

to Bruce,
for his love and support,
and for his helpful critique of the
manuscript of this book;

to Stuart R. Kaplan,
who never tried to cap my energies,
however eccentric a course they took;

to the Teachers,
who gave me the most precious gifts that can
be offered;

and to Norbert Lösche,
for creating the beautiful Cosmic Tarot.